ATTRACTING

MIRACLES

AND MY SECRET LIFE AS A MIRACLES COACH

GREGORY DOWNEY

WITH

DR. JOE VITALE

MOtivational PRESS®
LEADERS IN GLOBAL PUBLISHING

Published by Motivational Press, Inc.
1777 Aurora Road
Melbourne, Florida, 32935
www.MotivationalPress.com

Manufactured in the United States of America.

ISBN: 978-1-62865-343-4

CONTENTS

* * * * * * * *

ACKNOWLEDGEMENTS 5

FORWARD 7

PREFACE

THE AUTHOR'S TRUE CONFESSION 9

MIRACLE NUMBER 1

WHAT I DIDN'T WANT 13

MIRACLE NUMBER 2

WHAT I DID WANT 24

MIRACLE NUMBER 3

CLEARING MY LIMITING BELIEFS. 36

MIRACLE NUMBER 4

FEELING THINGS INTO EXISTENCE 54

MIRACLE NUMBER 5

LETTING GO 74

ATTRACTING MIRACLES

CONNECTING THE DOTS. 93

MY SECRET LIFE

A MIRACLES COACH 110

THE STORY OF MIRACLES COACHING°

BY DR. JOE VITALE. 122

APPENDIX

EXPERIENCE AN ATTRACTING MIRACLES

CONSULTATION: 127

ABOUT JERRY BORCHELT. 130

ACKNOWLEDGEMENTS

* * * * * * * *

THANK YOU TO MY FATHER, Dan Downey, for giving me the gift of life. The lessons I have learned from you along the way were hard. But learning them has made my life so much easier. I am who I am because you were willing to be who you were in spite of the challenges and the risks. I believe we will both come to see that what we experienced was perfect for both of us in the eyes of God. I'm grateful that all things between us have been resolved and that I can proudly call you Dad.

Thank you Hillary for believing in me, for loving me unconditionally, for being my warm, personal enemy, and also my truest friend. I look forward to eternity.

Thank you to my children, Asher, Caleb, Lila, Clarie, Eli, Samuel, and Brynna for bringing so much joy and learning to my life and for being 7 reasons to work hard and reach for the stars.

Thank you to my mother Leona Marino for being willing to have one more after the first experience with my brother Darin. And thank you for showing me that it's never too late to reach for your dreams. Your restaurant was fantastic!!!

Thank you to Peter and Judith Bellville (Mom and Dad B.) and the Bellville family for taking me in and making me a part of your tribe when it mattered most. I will forever be grateful for all you have done for me and for my family.

Thank you to Jerry Borchelt and Father John Crews for helping me to, "Get With The Program". You saved my life before it truly began.

Thank you to Justin Bellville, Jerry Moore, and Chad DeBie for treating me as a friend and brother.

Thank you Joe Vitale for creating Miracles Coaching and for showing me what is possible and always reminding me to expect miracles.

Thank you Adam Mortimer and Janeen Detrick for taking me under your wings and sharing so much of your knowledge and experience. You've helped me become an amazing coach.

Thank you to my publisher Motivational Press and to Justin Sachs for believing in my story and my mission even when I may have gotten a bit too big for my britches.

And to thank you to everyone else who has touched my life for good along the way.

FORWARD

* * * * * * * *

I'VE KNOWN GREGORY DOWNEY FOR at least half a decade. He is one of the personally trained coaches in my Miracles Coaching® program. Besides being a fellow book reader, and my interviewer every month for clients in Miracles Coaching®, he is my friend.

When Gregory told me he wanted to write a book, I urged him on. I knew his mountain of success stories with clients would be riveting. I knew his own story would be inspiring. What I didn't know is just how terrific his book would be.

He basically patterned his book after the five steps in my own bestselling book, *The Attractor Factor*. He took the basic formula but used his story and his experience to demonstrate how the formula works. The result is genius.

I found myself captivated by Gregory's life story. I found the stories of people he has coached to be enlightening, entertaining, and educational. I found the use of my five-step process as a framework for his book to be spectacular.

While it's always better to work directly with an experienced coach, the next best thing is to read this marvelous book by Gregory. You'll find it inspiring and informative. And it just might transform your life forever.

Turn the page and – Expect Miracles.

With Love,

Dr. Joe Vitale

Author of way too many books to list here

Founder and Creator, Miracles Coaching®

www.MrFire.com

PREFACE

THE AUTHOR'S TRUE CONFESSION

* * * * * * * *

MY LIFE WAS AN ABSOLUTE WRECK. And I'm not just saying that to grab your attention. It really was a wreck. I guess you could say that I had hit my rock bottom. And the truth is I hated myself for where I had ended up.

I was young, addicted, and at 18 years old, had absolutely no sense of direction for my life. Every new day was like the last, a struggle to get through the present one on to the next. But it was the nights that terrified me most. Because at night, when I would put my head on my pillow to fall asleep, that was when my father's voice would begin shouting all of the reminders of what I was and was not, and what I would never become. "You're a f-ing worthless piece of sh*t." "You'll never amount to anything". That wasn't even the worst of it. For several years I believed that I shouldn't even be alive.

I was fifteen years old the night he stopped his truck on the side of the road in Bodega Bay, California and in a drunken, drug fueled rage, put his gun to the side of my head and threatened to blow my brains out.

Although it wasn't the first time I feared he might actually kill me, it was the first time he had ever taken his threats to such an extreme. He told me several times during my childhood that no one gave a sh*t about me and that he would take me out in the back yard, shoot me and bury me and that no one would care. He said it was his right. He said he brought me into this world and he could take me out of it. And, well, when he put his gun to my head, I believed that was the moment he would make good on his promise.

Fortunately for both of us, things didn't go as badly as they could have. But, even though the gun never went off, something inside of me died on that terrifying night.

I walked about 25 miles that night looking for safety and shelter from the cold and pouring rain. The fact that no one would stop to give me a ride and that no one could see that I was hurting made his words true; every last one of them. "No one gives a sh*t about you". All of the walking, silence, loneliness, and the hurting drove the emotional nails even deeper into my coffin of limiting beliefs.

No matter how hard I tried over the next few years, I didn't know how to turn the voice off. But worse, I didn't know how to make him wrong when everything I was doing in my life seemed to make him right.

Fortunately, I eventually did learn how to turn the voice off. I also came to recognize that contrary to his claims, there were some people who actually did care about me. More importantly, there have been real miracles that have occurred in my life.

I hope you come to see that it's a miracle that you are holding this book in your hands. Most of all, the very fact that you are reading this book is proof positive that my father was and is and will forever be wrong about who I was, who I am, and who I will yet become.

Who am I? I AM Gregory Allan Downey. I AM a divine child of a living God. I AM a husband. I AM a lover. I AM a father. I AM a son. I AM a brother. I AM a friend. I AM an amazing man of light. I AM an agent of change. I AM an Attractor of Miracles. I AM a Miracles Coach.

As you read this book you will be encouraged to complete some exercises with the promise that if you follow through, you will experience specific results. You may not be able to see at first why you should do what I ask you to. You may doubt. You may question. You may over analyze. So, I want to encourage you to embrace these Four Laws of Learning that if followed, will result in countless miracles in your life and the lives of those you will influence for good. That is, if you choose to. And I believe that you will. Because I believe that like me, you are a seeker of truth and light.

Here are the four laws:

First: <u>Do it because I tell you to</u>. After all, I'm the coach right? And you are seeking miracles. Don't question it. Don't analyze it. Don't judge it. Just do it.

Second: <u>Do it because you see that it works</u>. As I have promised, you will begin to experience life-altering results by completing the exercises that are shared in this book. When you see that it works, you will want to do more of it. In this case, more is definitely better.

Third: <u>Do it because you know why it works</u>. As you experience results from completing the exercises in this book, eventually you will start to see the connection between each exercise and the law of attraction. When this happens, you will truly begin to become an awakened individual.

Fourth: <u>Share it</u>. As with anything else that you have experienced that has changed your life for good, you will develop the desire to share the principles in this book with others. Recognize that your desire to share is divinely inspired. Who knows? You may even feel called to become a personal development coach.

If at any point you cease to see miracles in your life, always remember what one of my mentors, K Michael Reid, has taught me. "The target doesn't move". If miracles cease, it's not because something has changed in the divine scheme of things. It's because you've strayed away from the process that allowed you to attract miracles in the first place. If that happens, go back to what worked and you will always regain the confidence that miracles are real and can happen for you.

May this book give you the courage, strength, and direction to manifest every miracle your heart desires from this day forward and forever.

Thank you to each person who has shown me that they really do care about me. And especially thank you to Jerry Borchelt; one of the greatest miracles that God ever graced me with. What you do to help the lost boys of Hanna Center truly does matter, sir. I understand you can't save them all. But you certainly helped to save this one. And so this book is dedicated to you - Oh Captain! MY Captain!

Thank you for reading.

Miraculously,

Gregory Downey

MIRACLE NUMBER 1

WHAT I DIDN'T WANT

❋   ❋   ❋   ❋   ❋   ❋   ❋   ❋

I ARRIVED AT HANNA BOYS CENTER in Sonoma, California already believing that I really didn't want to be there. Even though I had professed to the school's director that I did want to attend in my applicant interview, I was now being confronted by the reality of what lies ahead. After all, I was 13 years old, it was the middle of summer vacation, and once I checked in it meant that "My Freedom" would be taken from me for the foreseeable future, "Against My Will".

Hanna Boys Center is a therapeutic boarding school program designed to assist with boys who are considered to be "At Risk". Most of the boys enrolled at Hanna had long histories of adversity in their lives. The staff at Hanna believes that the key to recovery from those experiences was to build resilience. The program is designed to help boys develop strong, trusting relationships with caring adults, and to gain a sense of mastery in their lives, while helping families find ways to improve their relationships.

My father was an alcoholic, drug addict, and anger addict. He was verbally, emotionally, and at times very physically abusive. In all of my life I have never feared any human being in the same way that I feared my father. At 16 years old I got into a fist fight with a lineman for the local high-school football team. He was a year older, at least four inches taller than I was, and had about fifty pounds on me. However, in that very moment when I knew that a fight was going to happen with this kid that was built like a lumberjack, and I was going to be in it, I remained as cool as an autumn breeze. You see, I had been beat up pretty good by my father more times than I cared to count. My father had a large frame and was broad shouldered which was very imposing to a young man of 16 years old. So when it came time to fight, I just thought to myself, this guy isn't so big. How tough could he be? He certainly can't punch as hard as my father. I never waited around long enough to find out. When someone threatened me physically, I always made sure I took care of business as quickly as possible. I would swing hard, swing more than once, and always aim for the nose part of the face. You see, I got beat up plenty by my father at home. I didn't need to give that option to anyone else.

Because I had coppery red hair as a child, it was said by many in my family that I would grow up to have, "That hot Irish Temper." The subconscious mind responds to repetition and group identity (which is identifying with the actions or behaviors of a group). It's no wonder that by 7th grade I was expelled from school for getting in too many fights. And so, the "Best thing" for me was to be placed in a program that would get me the help I needed according too many including my father with all his issues.

Most reasonable people would think that I would have welcomed the separation from my father and the turmoil of living under his roof. And they might would be right in more ways than one. But, the unseen miracle behind my placement at Hanna Boys Center was that for the first time in my life, I actually started to consider what I didn't want. I didn't want to be away from the girl I had a crush on. I didn't want to give up fishing. I didn't want to give up weekends with Grandma and Grandpa Marino. I didn't want to give up smoking, drinking, and partying with friends, which I was already doing a lot. Most of all I didn't want to be controlled. And by this time, I was at an age where I could leave the house to avoid conflict, which minimized my run-ins with my father. So, the prospect of enduring his abuses on a more limited scale seemed acceptable to me at the time.

But this idea that there might be things that I actually didn't want in my life was a new concept. In my father's house, it didn't matter what I didn't want. In fact, what I thought or didn't think, what I felt or didn't feel, and what I believed or didn't believe was never even discussed. My father laid down the law. You didn't cry regardless of the circumstances. Even if he was beating you, you didn't cry. He would shout at you and tell you to stop crying or he would give you something to cry about, which made no sense to me since I was already crying because he was hitting me. This was the beginning of my inability to deal well with mixed messages later in life. Nonetheless, the law was made plain and you dared not go crossways with what he had established as law.

In his best selling audio program *The Abundance Paradigm*, my friend and mentor Dr. Joe Vitale introduces The First Step in the Law of Attraction as, "Know What You Don't Want."

So here I was, being dropped off at a residential treatment boarding school for the foreseeable future and right away I begin attracting miracles. For the first time in my life I'm actually consciously considering what I do not want in my life. In spite of the fact that the staff at Hanna could barely stand to deal with me because of my constant defiance to the center rules, this miracle in particular would lead to one of the most powerful lessons of my life time; "Being Clear About What I Don't Want Empowers Me To Choice." In my father's house I didn't have a lot of choice, and so here I was at 13 years old in an environment that was absolutely safe to act according to what I didn't want. There were consequences for my defiance, but, none of them included being yelled and cussed at, slapped, punched, being hit with an object, or having things thrown at me.

Anyone who was around during my stay at Hanna could tell you that in my first semester I was very vocal about and made numerous declarations about what I didn't want. So much so that they labeled me as "Not Getting With The Program." The last thing a staff member wants to hear is some smart-alecky kid going around telling everyone all day what they don't want to do, especially when, "Getting With The Program" includes a lot of doing what I was told to do by other people.

I have since had staff members tell me that I was one of the toughest cases they had seen come into the center when it came to not "Getting With The Program." During my stay at Hanna, if you didn't comply with what was being asked of you, you were given work detail by the hour. At one point, just prior to Christmas vacation, I had over 150 hours of work detail on the board. It was said by some of my peers and even by a few staff members that I had set a record for most hours earned in a single semester.

My caseworker, Ms. Mertens, certainly had her hands full with me. Fortunately, she was very nice and had the patience of a saint. Which made sense. After all, it was a Catholic program.

Despite what the staff at Hanna might have thought about me at the time, a miracle was happening right before their very eyes, even if they weren't aware of it. Their agenda was to get me to comply with the rules set out by Father Crews (the program director) and staff. However, for the first time in my life, God had placed me in an environment where I could actually express what I didn't want in my life and to do so with the sense of safety and security that I wasn't going to be physically, verbally, or emotionally abused for doing so. It felt terrific!

I recall something that I didn't want very clearly. I didn't want to be told that I couldn't smoke. So I went to great lengths to find places on campus where I could sneak away and enjoy uninterrupted time smoking one cigarette after another. I was never sure when I'd have another opportunity so I'd try to get through as many cigarettes as I could in one sitting. There was a group of trees next to the school building that concealed the opening to a culvert pipe. The pipe led to a small concrete chamber that was topped with a manhole cover beneath the lawn of the convent. On one occasion as I sat smoking in that concrete chamber, I pushed the manhole cover open just enough to pop my head out and scope out the situation. Sure enough, just as I did, one of the teacher's wives came driving in to bring her husband lunch. And there in the middle of the convent lawn, was the head of a wide-eyed middle-schooler topped with a manhole cover. We made direct eye contact. She knew exactly who it was, too. Amazingly, to her credit, she never did rat me out. My safe place would forever remain safe with her. I'm convinced it was because she didn't know what I was really up to that she kept quiet. She probably also knew I needed the space.

I was actually living the first step to attracting miracles. Of course, I didn't know it at the time. But I did know that it felt great to be free to express what I didn't want in my life. So I did it often, especially during those first few months at Hanna Boys Center.

Discovering what I didn't want led to a lot of adventure for me at Hanna. I didn't want to stay in the prescribed boundaries of the campus, so a lot of the time I didn't. Instead, I went hiking and exploring the oak covered hillsides and grassy fields that surrounded the wine country campus. At night, when it was lights out time, instead of sleeping I would hide beneath my blankets exploring the world of college radio. My favorite stations were KPFA at Cal Berkeley, KFJC at Foothill Junior College, and KUSF at the University of San Francisco. College radio unlocked my appetite for punk rock and other types of unique and independent alternative music that I still enjoy today. When the night watchman would come through, I would stay motionlessly beneath my blankets until I was sure he was far enough down the hall to be unaware of my stirring.

I don't share these things to brag about the open rebellion of youth, but to express the relief it was to finally be able to acknowledge and express what I didn't want in my life.

Knowing what I know now adds to the miracle of it all. In retrospect, I was clearly being prepared for my role as a Miracles Coach. Personal development is about becoming empowered, and if nothing else, at this point in my stay at Hanna, I was becoming empowered.

I've been a Miracles Coach now for a number of years. As a Miracles Coach, I work with clients from around the world and from all walks of life. I have engaged in thousands of coaching sessions with hundreds of clients. One of the topics I discuss in every first session with a client is the concept of, "Getting Clear About What You Don't Want." This comes across as counter intuitive to most clients, especially the ones who have studied personal development or the law of attraction for any amount of time. There seems to be this prevailing belief that mentioning what you don't want will somehow cause the universe to pour out a plague upon you and start sending you every last thing you're afraid of in large quantities. So it's important for me to remind them that, "Simply validating what you don't want isn't a promise or guarantee that you will perpetuate or bring more of the things that you don't want into your life."

The second prevailing myth among clients regarding what they don't want is that by validating the things they don't want in their life, they are somehow declaring that they are broken or defective. And so rather than bring the things they don't want to light, they often make every effort to distance themselves from those things; which in reality is much more likely to result in getting more of what they don't want in life. Trying to hide from or ignore the things they don't want is a resistance behavior. One of the most prevalent adages in personal development regarding the law of attraction is, "Whatever You Resist, Will Persist". By resisting the things that they don't want, coaching clients are almost insuring that they will continue to get more of it.

Everyone at some point in their life has to realize that there are things that they just don't want and that's okay. It's actually a necessary part of coming to enjoy real success and taking full advantage of the law of attraction.

I encourage every coaching client to write down the things they don't want. I want them to be as clear as they can about the things they either want to become free from or that they would like to stay free from. I've had some clients that describe life as a series of unwanted events that just keep happening over and over again. One client compared her life experience to that of a boxer living each day on the ropes. She went on to express how emotionally and physically exhausted she had become, feeling as though she had no real choice in life. Once she completed the assignment I gave her to list the things she didn't want, her life was forever changed. She saw she had a choice.

One of my closest friends, whom I also call my brother, Jerry, was working on a Master's of Fine Arts Degree from The University of Utah at the time we met. As we grew closer in our relationship, each of us being fathers, our conversations often turned to our hopes, dreams, and aspirations for our future. During one of our talks, I could tell that Jerry was deeply concerned about his future and how he feared that all of the time, energy, and resources that he was putting in to getting a master's degree in art may end up being somewhat of a waste. He confessed how it troubled him that he might never be able to do what he loved as a means to support his family. "What do you mean?" I asked. He went on to explain that there is prevailing belief in art academia that marketing your talents and having people actually buy your art work (at least while you are still living) is seen as *selling out* and is looked upon with disdain by many art academics. "Are you serious?" I asked. "Yeah. I'm serious." was his reply.

Jerry went on to explain how he had been involved in conversations with professors and other clients in his MFA program who had expressed contempt for artists who try to achieve some level of acclaim that goes beyond obscurity while they are still above ground and breathing. What bothered him most was that he was actually beginning to resign himself to that same school of thought. And it scared him.

As a result of subsequent conversations, Jerry began to get clear about what he didn't want. He didn't want to resign himself to teaching art in a college or university for low pay, he didn't want live out his life as an artist in obscurity, he didn't want to buy into the negative attitudes that seemed to be so prevalent in art academia, and he certainly didn't want to be a "Starving Artist" his entire life. So I basically said, "Then don't. Choose to follow your passion instead." From then on Jerry began using his 'don't want list' to push him in the direction of his dreams and goals.

Today my friend Jerry owns an art school just outside of Houston, Texas and is actively creating and selling his artwork. One thing he does especially well is portraiture. Jerry can take individual pictures of people that they like and combine them in to a group portrait. Now that's talent.

One of my Miracles Coaching clients, Emmerl, wrote to me in an email about her experience with getting clear about her don't wants:

"I am now more skilled at knowing what I don't want. As a result, I am much more clear about what has been holding me back."

Another Miracles Coaching Client named Vanina shared how she reconnected with a part of her that she had lost touch with:

"With the help of my coach, I have been able to once again get clear about what I don't want. I don't want to work a dead end job! I had become so accustomed to doing whatever has been required to maintain a basic existence; I had forgotten what it's like to dream of a more prosperous life."

I encourage you to take some time and list out the top 10 to 15 things you don't want in your life. Listing what you don't want is what I refer to as The First Fork in the Road To Empowerment. You become empowered when you choose to stay off of the road that leads to more of what you don't want.

By listing the things you don't want in life, you are in essence drawing a line in the sand. You are making your declaration of ownership of your life. Your declaration might sound something like this, "From this day forward, I will fearlessly acknowledge the things that I DO NOT Want in my life and I choose to forever turn away from the that road which leads to getting more of the things that I have confidently declared that I Do NOT Want."

Now is the perfect time to make a commitment to yourself that you will sit down and make your Don't Want list. Don't question it. Just do it. Joe Vitale has taught me on many occasions that, "The Universe Loves Speed." Meaning, don't hesitate and don't wait around. Take action. If you feel inspired to make your list, give in to that inspiration. The longer you wait to take action, the weaker the urge to act will become, which means the easier it will be to put it off long enough to lose desire all together. Hesitation to do this exercise is almost guaranteed to keep you from moving forward and attracting the miracles you deserve to experience in your life.

Once you have your list of Don't Wants, go through it and ask the following question for each item on the list; "Why am I still dealing with that?" You will want to write down the answer in the form of a statement. For example, if you don't want to be surrounded by negative people but you find that there are negative people wherever you go, you would say, "Everyone around me is negative." Remember, this is a statement of belief and may not necessarily be the truth. It may appear to be true to you, but in reality is just a belief.

Once you complete this exercise, you will want to set aside your list and the answers to the follow-up questions for later.

I will explain what to do with this information in a coming chapter.

It took me years to discover the real power that came in knowing what I didn't want. Looking at my life now, it's quite clear the powerful role that this principle has played in my life. I decided I didn't want to be an alcoholic, drug addict, or anger addict. I decided I didn't want to beat my wife or my children. I didn't want my family to fear for their physical safety when I was present. I didn't want my wife or kids to feel worthless. I didn't want to feel worthless. I didn't want to be a nobody. I didn't want to be average. I didn't want to remain silent.

Choosing what I didn't want meant taking complete responsibility for my life. This meant no excuses. I would look at anything that needed to be addressed and I would take it head on. It hasn't always been the easiest thing in the world. But, declaring what I don't want has empowered me to choose."

As I said before, getting clear about what you don't want can sometimes be a challenge. But in the end, it can also give you the courage to become empowered and to clearly identify what you do want.

Miracle Number 2

What I Did Want

* * * * * * * *

H<small>E NEVER WORE A GOATEE</small> like he did today when I attended his homeroom class. He just wore a thick Tom Selleck style mustache and a hair-style that I thought was a bit plain, almost folksy. He looked like he could have been a member of any of the more popular folk bands of the 70's. And he had the guitar playing skills to match.

You'd never guess by looking at him now that he ever had so much hair. The years have added character to his appearance. Still, every weekday Jerry Borchelt makes the fifteen minute drive from his home in Sonoma to the campus of Arch Bishop Hanna School for Boys. It's the same drive he's made for over forty years.

Each day his focus is placed on the same thing, to inspire the boys of Hanna Boys Center to become not just educated, but to become someone who uses their brain to think and to question and to understand the deeper meaning of things.

I'll never forget the day he asked me to come into his classroom during lunchtime. This meant giving up time at the rec. center playing pool or foosball or doing something else that would clearly lead to a more promising future; like watching tv or hiding out and smoking cigarettes in the equipment closet behind the rec. center as some of us boys were known to do. But this day would be different. It's important to point out that it was just before Christmas vacation or Christmas home visit as it was called.

Mr. Borchelt, or Mr. B as I affectionately called him, never did things without a good reason. This particular day, his intention was to determine my current reading level in hopes that he could use the results to make a point with me. He had a box that had cards with passages from various literary works. He would hand me a card, ask me to read through it and then asked me to answer a series of questions about what I had just read. After reading about 5 or 6 of these cards and answering the questions posed he determined that I was reading at about university level. Then he stared at me for a moment in silence. I wasn't yet "Getting With The Program" and he knew it. There were no secrets about a boy's performance across the board at Hanna Center.

The way that discipline was served at Hanna was through hours of physical labor. During the time of our visit I had accrued over 150 work hours. It bothered Mr. B that I wasn't "Getting With The Program". "How are you going to work all of those off?" he asked. "I don't know," I said. He looked right at me shaking his head and said, "What a waste." Mr. B. didn't pull any punches. He just said it like it was – even if it smacked you right between the eyes.

It especially bothered Father Crews, the program director, that I wasn't "Getting With The Program". Together, he and Mr. B. would stand on the steps overlooking the school-yard and wonder aloud to each other, "When is he going to GET IT?" Fortunately for me, this day would be that day.

As we sat there in near silence, he stared across the table at me for a moment or two, then he said, "Just as I thought. You're brilliant. You don't even know how brilliant you are, do you? No one has ever told you."

We talked somewhat about my life back at home and the messages I received from my father. He then took an index card and wrote the words "Carpe Diem" and slid the card toward me across the table. I reached out and took the card and stared at it blankly. "Do you know what that means?" he asked? "No I don't." I replied. "It's Latin." He said. "It says Seize The Day. You have the power to Make Each Day a Masterpiece."

I cried. I wasn't sure why at the time. But I cried. This was the first time in my life anyone had told me I had the power to choose anything. Mr. B. was telling me that I had the power to choose whatever I wanted my life to be, whatever I wanted to learn or whatever I wanted to become. It was up to me to choose.

He got up and deliberately walked across the classroom to his desk. He opened a drawer, took something out of it, and came back to the table where I was sitting. He reached his hand out, offering me a book. I took the book from his hand. I looked at the front cover. It was a book I had never heard of.

"I think you should read it," he said. "Okay," I replied. "It's called *Jonathan Livingston Seagull*," he said. By now I was curious about this book with a sketch of a seagull in flight on the front cover.

That afternoon, when school let out, I took the book with me to my dorm and began to read.

———

Jonathan Livingston Seagull, written by Richard Bach, is a fable about a seagull learning about life and flight, and a homily about self-perfection. It was first published in 1970 as *Jonathan Livingston Seagull — a story*. By the end of 1972, over a million copies were in print.

Jonathan is a seagull who is bored with daily squabbles over food among the other seagulls. Seized by a passion for flight, he pushes himself, learning everything he can about flying, until finally, his unwillingness to conform results in his expulsion. An outcast, he continues to learn, becoming increasingly pleased with his abilities as he leads a peaceful and happy life.

One day, Jonathan is met by two gulls who take him to a "higher plane of existence." A better world found through the pursuit of higher knowledge. There he meets other gulls who love to fly. He discovers that his sheer tenacity and desire to learn make him "pretty well a one-in-a-million bird." In this new place, Jonathan befriends the wisest gull, Chiang, who takes him beyond his previous learning, teaching him how to move instantaneously to anywhere else in the universe. The secret, Chiang says, is to "begin by knowing that you have already arrived."

So, basically Jonathan learns that the secret to an extraordinary existence is to first 'Choose What You Want'.

By handing me the index card with the words Carpe Diem, by admonishing me to "Make Each Day A Masterpiece", by having me read *Jonathan Livingston Seagull*, Mr. Borchelt was teaching me to claim my 'Power to Choose What I Did Want'. This was The Second Miracle.

Hanna Boys Center had a policy that was itself a sort of Godsend. Father Crews was a man that believed in repentance and second chances. Little did I know that when a boy returned home from Christmas Break all of his work detail hours were wiped completely clean, erased, remitted, and forgiven. In short, all of my free time would once again become my own. This was a beautiful thing because as I watched my father drive up the long driveway from the highway to the administration building, I made a vow to myself that when I returned from Christmas Break, I would, "Get With The Program."

I had decided that if I ever hoped to finish school, have a girlfriend, hang out with my friends, and take back my life, I would have to graduate from the program. This meant I would first need to, "Get With The Program." I say this at the risk of sounding ungrateful for my time at Hanna Center, which I should emphasize, is not the case.

At Mr. B.'s nudging, I would go on to read a number of books over the latter half of that first year. *The Catcher in the Rye, Les Miserables,* and *The Count of Monte Cristo* were all on the list. Each one of them deals with individuals making profound and life changing decisions about what they did want in their lives. But, none of them would ever be as meaningful as or more profound than *Jonathan Livingston Seagull.* I think mostly because I could tell that Mr. B. saw Jonathan Livingston Seagull in me. For that I was touched and a bit flattered. I was being told that I was something or someone special.

In his best seller *The Attractor Factor,* Joe Vitale lists, "Know What You Do Want" as Step #2 in the Law of Attraction process. Knowing what you want places you in a position of choice. As a Miracles Coach I share a principle with my clients called 'The Road To Empowerment'.

On 'The Road to Empowerment' there exists a fork. The path to the left offers a journey toward what you don't want. The path to the right offers a journey toward what you do want. All of my clients are asked to make two lists. The first, as you recall from the previous chapter, is a list of 10 to 15 things that they Don't Want in their life. The second is a list of 10 to 15 things that they Do Want. By listing your Don't Wants and Do Wants you create a visual representation of each path.

In the timeless classic, *Alice's Adventures in Wonderland*, Alice comes to a fork in the path on which she is walking. Near the path in a tree sat the Cheshire Cat. Upon spotting the cat, Alice engages it in the following conversation:

Alice: Would you tell me, please, which way I ought to go from here?

The Cheshire Cat: That depends a good deal on where you want to get to.

Alice: I don't much care where.

The Cheshire Cat: Then it doesn't much matter which way you go.

Alice: ...So long as I get somewhere.

The Cheshire Cat: Oh, you're sure to do that, if only you walk long enough."

I have had more clients than I can count that start our time together describing life as a series of events that had happened to them. They tell me how they have lived their life reacting to things that come their way, never feeling as though they have any choice.

As their coach, it's my responsibility to help my clients fully recognize their situation and to also help them take responsibility for where they are in that moment. On occasion I'm met with resistance from clients who are reluctant to own the results of their decisions or lack of decision. Until they own where they are in life, they are destined to remain stuck creating more of what they don't want. It usually doesn't take very long for them to make the necessary adjustment in their thinking and to move forward taking 100% responsibility for their life.

Unfortunately we live in a time and place where far too often people blame their circumstances as the cause of their failure or lack of happiness. Maybe you're that type of person. And even if you're not, I'm sure you know a few. It's this type of person that has a tendency to view life as a series of negative experiences that happen "to them" rather than viewing life's experiences as something they create or things that happen "for them".

Allow me to explain in more detail.

From the fourth grade on I had a close friend named Mike who had a habit of borrowing my things for extended periods of time. When I would ask for them back, he would look at me with an expression of reluctance and inquire, "Why should I?" To which I would reply, "Because it's mine, that's why." To which he would respond smugly, "Possession is 9/10 of the law." Meaning, because it's in his possession he could do whatever he wanted with it and there wasn't much I could do to prove it was mine.

This behavior drove me absolutely nuts because deep down there was an element of truth to what he was saying. I would later come to find out that he did this as a means of feeling empowered through exercising control over my things. And although I hated it at the time, eventually I came to see this principle of possession being 9/10 of the law as one of the most powerful principles in personal development.

A person's circumstances are what they are because they have allowed them to be what they are. And whether they have done it consciously or not, they have created their circumstances through their beliefs and the choices they have made over time. This is a hard reality for some people to accept. Most would rather blame something outside themselves than accept responsibility for where they are in life. Maybe it's just easier that way. By not accepting responsibility, they are actually professing that they are powerless to take control over the things that lead to their unhappiness and to change their life into something not just worth living, but worth living happily.

I recently had an acquaintance confide in me that she had been struggling for a number of years from the effects of an abusive marriage. She was depressed and miserable, and spending countless hours with a therapist who was doing nothing more than validating the victim position and prolonging this lady's unhappiness.

This lady was blaming her current circumstances on something that was no longer a part of her life. In fact, she had actually moved on and left the marriage several years previous. The whole marriage situation was In The Past, yet she continued to wallow in her miserable circumstances. CIRCUMSTANCES... What are they? They are the "Things Standing Around You." Imagine your life being like a canvas and your circumstances being the colors and images on that canvas. Each and every day we are given the opportunity to paint our canvas in a way that we feel is best for us. Granted, some have more training in the art of living than others. But everyone has the equal opportunity to learn to be a better painter, a better creator of circumstances.

Sometimes in life others may come along with their paintbrush and either add color to that canvas or place big black marks right in the middle. A mark that not only covers some of the beauty that we had previously painted but that stands out so much that it makes it very difficult to recognize the beautiful colors elsewhere on the canvas. Did we ask for them to place that mark there? Absolutely not. Do we want that mark there? Absolutely not. But do we own it? Absolutely! Remember, "Possession is 9/10 of the law." You see, once a stroke is left on the canvas of our life whether we asked for it or not, it is ours and we now have complete responsibility for what happens with it. We can either leave it there, pointing at it and proclaiming our disgust, all the while asking others to do something with it for us. Or, we can choose to act. Because the truth is, we own it! Which means we have permission and power to remove it from our life and replace it with something that we truly want there instead. This can be done through the clearing process. Clearing is like removing the unwanted black marks and allowing the beauty that lies beneath to be brought to the surface. I'll speak more on this in the next chapter.

Who would have guessed that a statement I absolutely detested in my youth would come to serve so many, myself included, in such a positive way? I challenge you to own and address the many black marks on your canvas. Let them know that you are aware of their presence. But also let them know that you do not intend to keep them there and as the owner of your canvas, you refuse to allow them to be a part of your circumstances. I challenge you to say it out loud. There is real power in the spoken word. Then choose each day to replace those unwanted, hurtful, scary things with something beautiful, enlightening, and inspiring. Eventually there will be no room in your life for the black marks and they will all be released through the clearing process.

Taking 100% responsibility for where you are and what you want in your life today is a core part of creating the life you truly desire. Because only then can you choose where you will be the next day and the next day and the next day, until you have arrived at your ideal set of circumstances.

It may take awhile, for some longer than others. But when you arrive at that place where you are fully empowered and claim ownership of your circumstances and your future, then and only then, can you look in the mirror and with all sincerity and conviction proclaim yourself the creator of all that you desire.

Each of us has the power to choose what we want and which direction we will go in life. In fact, it's our responsibility and no one else's to choose which way we will go at the fork in the road. We can either take the path that leads to more of what we don't want or the one that offers what we do want. Life often gives us situations that are challenging and painful. We're left with two choices. We can point the finger and complain, staying stuck in our story, or we can choose to own our power to change it.

One Miracles Client named Thomas shared the power of getting clear about his Do Wants:

"Over the last 3 months working with you as my coach, we focused on the Law of Attraction and you helped me find some clarity regarding what I want in my life. We then were able to uncover some of my Limiting Beliefs around money,

work, and delegation of tasks to others. One major Belief that we came up was the belief that I have to do everything myself and I cannot trust others to help me. By identifying this Limiting Belief and realizing that I want more for myself than what I'm currently getting, I was then able to do some clearing exercises to eliminate the belief and then take action in the direction of my goal by delegating to others."

I encourage you to take some time and list the things that you want in life. I recommend listing 10 to 15 items. Focus on the things that would make the most positive difference in your life.

Once you have made your Do Want List, go though it and ask yourself the following question for each item on the list; "Why haven't I manifested that in my life yet?" As you consider the answer to each of the questions, write the answer on your pieces of paper in statement form. For example, if you want a million dollars in your bank account and you ask yourself, "Why haven't I manifested that yet", the answer may be, "The economy stinks". Write down on your paper, "I don't have a million dollars in my bank account because the economy stinks."

You may recall from the last chapter that the answers to your questions about what you don't want in your life are the beliefs behind why you haven't gotten free from those issues. Similarly, the answers to the follow-up questions in this exercise are the beliefs behind why you haven't yet manifested the things you desire on your Do Want list. It's important to clearly list the answers. You will want to refer to the answers from both exercises in the next chapter.

The answers that you wrote down for each of the listing exercises are what are called, "Limiting Beliefs". Whether the statements of belief are true or not, they are true to you. The fact that they are true to you is what allows them to prevent you from freeing yourself from the things that you don't want and from manifesting the things that you do want. It is limiting beliefs that keep people stuck in mediocrity and dissatisfaction. The key to getting un-stuck is being able to break though the limiting belief; which you can. I have helped hundreds of people to get free from the limiting beliefs that keep them stuck.

MIRACLE NUMBER 3

CLEARING MY LIMITING BELIEFS

❧   ❧   ❧   ❧   ❧   ❧   ❧   ❧

As you might have guessed, I finally "Got With The Program". I graduated from Hanna Boys Center and regained what any fifteen year-old boy wants more than anything, "Freedom". Leaving the program meant returning to live in my father's house. But, I wouldn't return to school with old friends from elementary school. Instead, I went on to attend high school at Justin Siena, an upscale Catholic Prep School in Napa California. Yes! It's a fact. I had earned an academic scholarship toward the finest education that money could buy. The people who knew me declared this to be the miracle of miracles. I had always done so poorly in school until my time at Hanna. I still wouldn't believe it to this day if I hadn't actually lived it.

Going back to live in my father's house meant going back to the same chaos as before. It also meant some new chaos. You see, unfortunately while I was away working on improving myself and coming to a deeper understanding of who I was and who I wanted to become in my life, my father was on autopilot, living day in and day out the same as he had before. Wake up, go to work, come home, start drinking until bed time, and then off to bed to rest up for another go round the next day. He would drink double duty on the weekends.

I was almost two years older, I had grown a few inches taller, and the dynamic between him and I had changed considerably. He wasn't as quick to get physical with me unless he had been drinking. He certainly still found ways to tear me apart verbally. He would say things like, "I'll take you out in the back yard and shoot you and bury you and no one would even give a sh*t. It's my right. You worthless piece of sh*t." He was always quick to remind me that, "You don't live here. You're just visiting." or "Nobody even wants you around. I sure as sh*t don't. It's too bad they didn't keep you out there." ('There meaning Hanna Center'). "Maybe I'll drop you're a** back off out there - punk."

The fact is, he couldn't send me back. Although there were times I wish I could have gone back. But the truth is, I had done everything I needed to do while at Hanna Center to become a "Normal" functioning member of society, and probably more highly functioning than most kids my age. I was certainly more emotionally intelligent and possessed wisdom beyond my 15 years.

He often got home from work and started drinking before I could get home from school. His new game was to keep the door to the living room open slightly, just enough to hear me walk across the gravel from the street to the carport. He'd then quickly move from the living room and position himself in the laundry area of our kitchen. When I'd come in to the house through the door into the kitchen, he would try to surprise me with a smack upside the head before I could see it coming. It worked only a handful of times before I developed super human reflexes and was able to duck and dodge then slip past him, dart through the house, and out the back door.

I managed to keep as much distance between us as possible and to stay away from the house as long as I possibly could. Most of the time, I never went home for dinner and stayed out until nearly bedtime. Even though I was hungry a lot of the time at school, I liked it better than being in his house. I think he liked it better that way as well.

Not having the support I needed at home made doing homework and getting good grades nearly impossible. My overall academic performance was average at best. My instructors could tell that I was "Extremely Bright". My classroom participation demonstrated a solid grasp of the material and my exam scores were exceptional. Unfortunately, it wasn't enough to maintain the type of grades I had been earning at Hanna.

I had more than one instructor that wanted to help me to perform at my full ability. Unfortunately, I didn't know how to explain my situation at home, so I made excuses for my poor performance. This often resulted in a feeling of humiliation. I wanted so desperately to do better. I just didn't know how in light of the circumstances.

Attending an expensive prep school in California's Wine Country was a bit of a double-edged sword. I made a lot of new friends and was afforded a number of opportunities that could never be matched by attending the local public high school. Yet the fact that I was there on scholarship and not of the same socio-economic class was known by many if not all of the other students in my grade and many in the grades above me. There were some that were quick to point this out, which just added to my limiting beliefs. I didn't feel that I fit in or that I as good enough to be there or even deserved to be on the same campus as the "Rich Kids of Justin Siena". That first year at Justin Siena offered a number of tests both on campus and off.

My public school friends harassed me for going to Catholic school. They accused me of believing I was suddenly something I wasn't or that I was now "Too good" to go to public school. They were also quick to remind me of my working class roots. They either couldn't or wouldn't understand that I just wanted the opportunity to do and be more than I could be if I found my way back to the rut I was in before Hanna.

Looking back on it, it is apparent that they, too, had their own share of limiting beliefs. They were just more generous with theirs. Eventually it made sense to limit my exposure to those who didn't seem to have my best interest at heart.

As I struggled to navigate my way though the maze of adversity, there was no possible way to see or anticipate the events that were to occur along a narrow and winding stretch of Highway 1 just outside the sleepy bayside town of Bodega Bay, California. It was an event however, that would leave me nearly indomitable in the face of all other future adversity.

It was shortly after 2:00am on that insane Friday night. We left The Dry Dock Pizzaria at closing time. He was as drunk as I'd ever seen him but he didn't ask me to drive. Not this time. Instead I just sat in the passenger seat of his truck, wondering how we were going to make it back to the campground where we had parked the boat earlier that evening.

The night air was chilly, the fog was thick, and it was drizzling. So I didn't think walking was such a good idea. The

California Coast in mid November bears its own special brand of meteorological misery. Then again, getting in a vehicle with someone that had been drinking for the past 6 hours probably wasn't a major display of genius by any stretch. Either way, my safety would run out shortly and I was in for a really long night.

We drove less than a mile and then it happened. He just stopped the truck in the middle of the Pacific Coast Highway, and out came the gun. In a drunken and drug fueled rage he clumsily reached toward me and placed it against the side of my head and threatened to blow my brains out. All I could think was, "This is not happening. Oh sh*t! Yes! Yes it is happening. And this is where it all ends for me."

Although it wasn't the first time I believed he might kill me, it was the first time he ever took his threats to such an extreme. He had told me several times that no one gave a sh*t about me and that he would take me out in the back yard and shoot me and bury me and no one would care. And, well, I believed that this was the moment he would make good on his promise.

He just started shouting "Get out!!! Get the F- out of here!!! Punk ass!!! Run!!! Sissy!!!" I certainly wasn't stupid enough to just sit there. So I did exactly what he told me to do. I got out of the truck as quickly as I could. And then I ran.

I was filled with terror and anticipation, wondering when I'd hear the crack from the muzzle and feel the bullet rip through my flesh and lodge inside me: A single bullet that would start the bleeding and drain me of my life. But they never came, neither sound nor bullet.

I thought the way I was running would take me up the side of a grassy hill. It turned out to be a sloped thorn bush that was growing up out of a deep ravine. I went to step "Up Hill" but fell down through the bushes to the bottom of the ravine. You can imagine my surprise when my feet didn't find solid ground.

The ground was rocky and thorny where I hit bottom and it hurt something awful. I hit the side of my head on a rock. But, I didn't dare let out a sound. I feared he might be outside of the truck looking for me. I just lay in motionless silence listening to the hush of the ocean waves off in the distance for what felt like an eternity. Then finally, I heard the truck slip into gear and I breathed a sigh of relief in time with the whine of the truck's motor as he drove off into the darkness of that horrifying fog covered night.

Thank God he didn't find me. Thank God for misplaced feet. Thank God for the thorn bushes and the mud and the rocks. Thank God I was alive! I was alive! I gladly welcomed a few rocks and thorns over what could have been a single bullet that would have ended my life.

When I felt it was safe enough to climb out of the ravine and figure out what to do next, I began to make that painful yet fateful climb back up to the highway.

The ground was wet and slippery and the only things to grab onto were the thorn-covered branches of the bushes that concealed my temporary resting place. Every effort to pull myself up was excruciating. Part of me wanted to just lay back down there forever. But the better part of me - the part that God placed within me to guide me though troubled waters - was calling me upward, back toward the distant lights of the harbor, to begin the journey that would take me across the dark and perilous waters of addiction and despair, studying, learning, applying, and overcoming.

When I finally made it back up to the road, it was still foggy, raining, and cold. The truck was nowhere to be seen. So I began walking.

I spent the next ten or so miles walking and picking thorns out of my hands with a pocketknife. What would happen from here? Where would I go? Where would I live? I knew I couldn't stay in his home. The whole thought of it just didn't feel safe anymore. And I certainly never felt welcome anyway. He always reminded me that I didn't live there; I was just visiting. But none of that mattered in the moment. I had to keep walking. I had to get out of the rain and the cold. More importantly, I had to make it to somewhere that I could feel safe. After all, I had just nearly been taken from this world.

It was the weekend before Thanksgiving and to this day I am grateful that he didn't pull the trigger of his gun; that in and of itself was its own special miracle. I don't know why he didn't shoot. No one was around to witness anything and he was certainly drunk and drugged up enough to disregard the consequences. After all these years, the only thing I can come up with is that there must have been some unseen force that overcame him or perhaps the gun just simply malfunctioned. I have no idea which. I walked nearly 25 miles that night terrified and confused, trying to make sense of my life up until that point.

The fact that no one would stop to give me a ride and that no one could see that I was hurting made his words true; every last one of them. "No one gives a sh*t about you." All of the walking, silence, loneliness, and the hurting drove the emotional nails even deeper into my coffin of limiting beliefs.

By sun up I finally managed to catch a ride with a guy who was commuting to work. As luck would have it, we were both headed close to the same place. I explained that I had been walking from Bodega Bay since about 2:30am. He was nice enough to give me a ride all the way to where I was headed. It ended up only being about ten minutes out of his way.

It was nearly 10am when I finally arrived at the one place I thought I could go to sort things out. I knocked on the garage door for what seemed like an hour. She finally woke up, opened the door, and let me in. "What are you doing here?" she asked. "I thought you were at Bodega with your father," she continued. "You're not going to believe this," I said. "Believe what?", she asked. So, I explained what had happened in the early hours of that morning and how I had walked to Santa Rosa from Bodega Bay then managed to hitch a ride the rest of the way, and why I was now at her house.

It turns out I was right. She didn't believe me. In fact, she later confessed that she thought I had made it all up because she didn't want it to be real. If it was real, then she would have to do something about it and she didn't really know what she could do. And so, it was just easier to pretend it wasn't real.

She was gracious enough to let me get some sleep. I certainly needed it. Once I lay down it didn't take long for me to drift into unconsciousness.

I slept hard until early evening. I might as well have been asleep for the next 5 years. When I finally awoke, the previous night's events, although just a memory, crowded my mind like an army of well-placed scarecrows.

It didn't take long to realize that I was unable to erase the memories. Nor was I able to just push them aside. So, I did the only thing that made sense at the time and that was to fight fire with fire. I began my journey on another road; a road that led to alcohol, drugs, and reckless abandon. I used the same weapons that caused my pain in an effort to fight it.

The next 5 years was one of the most difficult periods of my life. No matter how hard I tried, nothing worked out for me. It seemed like the harder I tried, the worse things became.

I was young, addicted, and at 18 years old had absolutely no sense of direction for my life. Every new day was like the last, a struggle to get through the present day and on to the next. But it was the nights that terrified me most. Because at night, when I would put my head on my pillow to fall asleep was when my father's voice would begin shouting all of the reminders of what I was and was not, and what I would never become. "You're an f-ing worthless piece of sh*t." "You'll never amount to anything."

It was a fact. I had nothing to show for all my efforts. I drifted from one failure to the next. Each failure was just another rock on the growing pile that would eventually become the monument to my father's prediction for my life. I had all but come to the conclusion that he was right. I would really amount to nothing. I have to admit that I was absolutely terrified by the thought of it. So much so that the very idea of living as a 'nothing' nearly led me to take my own life. How could I remain in a life that had so much to offer and not be allowed to enjoy any of it? But, instead I chose the slow path to suicide - drugs and alcohol.

Through the darkness there would sometimes come tiny rays of light. I would hear Jerry Borchelt's voice reminding me that I was meant for greatness and that I could make each day a masterpiece; but how? Every effort ended in failure. Even the smallest successes seemed to be short lived. I so desperately needed guidance. It was very obvious that I wasn't finding what I needed on my current path. So, I did what any desperate person might think to do. I prayed.

In the depths of my despair, in the dark of night, as I lay awake in bed tormented by the reality of my situation, I reached out to God for help. I literally prayed out loud and asked God for direction. In that same prayer I promised that if I could be shown how to fulfill my potential that I would follow whatever path God opened up before me.

For me, hitting rock bottom gave me something solid to begin building on. After all, when you're down as far as I had been, they say the only direction to go is up.

In just over 4 years time, my life turned around nearly completely. In fact, I found myself on what proved to be a very unlikely path. This new path led me to sobriety, spirituality, a two-year church mission, and a passion for personal development. I met the woman of my dreams, got married, went to college, started a family, and embarked on a sacred mission to heal the emotional hurts of my fellow human beings. Today I get to help people unleash their greatness and attract miracles through personal coaching. It's funny that if you had told me four years prior that I would wake up one day and find myself in similar, if not the exact circumstances I was in by that time, I would have probably smacked you in the head for being a wise guy.

But it was true. Every bit of it was true. The only way to describe it is that I had been reinvented. I had put my entire life behind me, in nearly every sense, and began living a life of my choosing. I was no longer a victim nor would I ever allow myself to be one ever again. I had learned to take 100% responsibility for my life and my circumstances.

Although I very literally no longer resembled my past self, life wasn't totally void of challenges. I was still battling my limiting beliefs. I regularly heard my father's voice reminding me that in spite of all of my triumphs, I was still - at my core - worthless. But, in spite of the limiting beliefs, I was gaining ground, and life was becoming everything I desired to become.

Joining Joe Vitale's Miracles Coaching Team marked a major shift in my career as a personal development coach as well as a shift in my own understanding and practice of personal development. Prior to this quantum leap, clarity simply meant knowing in exact detail the things that I wanted to Be, Do, and Have in my life. It wasn't until my relationship with Joe and his two top coaches at the time (Janeen Detrick and Adam Mortimer) that I began to learn the deeper meaning of "Getting Clear". In the Miracles Coaching program we call it, "Clearing Limiting Beliefs."

Clearing Limiting Beliefs is the process of ridding your subconscious mind or your inner being of the emotional and energetic attachments to beliefs that don't serve your higher good. Clearing Limiting Beliefs is done by applying one or more clearing methods.

I was first introduced to Joe Vitale through the world of affiliate marketing. Aside from being a Law of Attraction guru, Joe is a master copywriter and internet marketer. Not to mention he is the author of too many books to list. It was through Joe Vitale and his best selling book *The Attractor Factor* that I was first introduced to the concept of clearing limiting beliefs.

Before Joe Vitale, personal development was mostly about time management, goal setting, repeating affirmations, getting and staying motivated, vision boards, and positive thinking.

Imagine that inside your mind exists a balance scale like the one represented on the statue of Lady Justice. On one side of the balance are stacked gold bars. On the other side are stacked lead bricks. Goal setting, repeating affirmations, making vision boards, and positive thinking are all activities that can be compared to adding gold bars to the one side of your balance. On the other side lies the lead bricks that represent limiting beliefs.

While most people who are actively engaged in personal development spend most of their time stacking gold bars on to their balance, the vast majority remain unaware of the lead bricks that weigh down the other side of their balance. In fact, most personal development gurus do very little if anything at all to address the concept of limiting beliefs. Even though I was aware that I had beliefs about myself that were holding me back from achieving my true potential, the notion of somehow getting free from those beliefs had never even crossed my mind. Instead, my beliefs about success and how it is achieved were made up of all of the various ways one could add more gold bars to their mental balance. Looking back on my personal development journey, I often wonder how much time I would have spent working to reach even equity between gold and lead had I never discovered Clearing Limiting Beliefs. It's important also to recognize that while I made a daily effort to pile gold on to my balance, the notion that I could spend an equal or greater amount of time removing lead from the opposing side never even crossed my mind. In fact, I had just viewed the entire endeavor as an effort to pile on as much gold as possible.

Spending time with Joe, Janeen, and Adam, and studying Joe's books and audio courses not only opened my mind to a vast set of new tools to begin clearing my own limiting beliefs, it further equipped me to assist hundreds of coaching clients world wide to break free from their limiting beliefs once and for all.

Clearing limiting beliefs can be broken down into five simple but effective steps.

Step number 1: <u>Identify The Limiting Belief</u>.

The easiest method that I share with my coaching clients to identify their limiting beliefs can be summed up in a review of chapters one and two of this book. First, make a list of 10 to 15 things you don't want in your life and second, make a list of 10 to 15 things you do want in your life. Once you've made your don't want list, it's important to ask yourself, "Why am I not free from the things I don't want?" The answer to the question, whether it sounds like a reason or an excuse, is generally the belief behind the issue that is preventing you from ridding your life of the items on your list.

After you've completed your list of things that you do want, you should ask yourself, "Why haven't I manifested those things in to my life?" Again, the answer to the question is generally the belief that is holding you back from manifesting the items on your list.

Another simple way to identify limiting beliefs is by becoming aware of *Counter Intentions*. *Counter Intentions* are actions and behaviors that are not in alignment with your desired outcomes or *Intentions*. Understand that we don't act according to what we desire. We act according to what we believe about what we desire. If your beliefs are out of alignment with your desires, the result will be *Counter Intentions*. Take some time to examine the areas of your life that are plagued by *Counter Intentions*. Write them down. Then ask yourself, "If there is a benefit to acting in this way, what is it?" The perceived benefit to acting counter to your desired outcome is the belief behind the *Counter Intention*. Be sure to write the belief down. You'll need it in the following step.

Step number 2: <u>Identify and measure the feeling that is attached to or giving energy to the limiting belief</u>.

By measuring the feeling on a scale from 1 to 10, you can quickly identify the level of emotional energy that is associated with the limiting belief.

An easy way to measure the feeling is to close your eyes and look downward toward your naval. While placing your attention on your naval, state the belief out loud 3 to 4 times giving yourself enough time in between statements to observe any feelings that might come to the surface. Should any feeling surface, make a mental note of the intensity of the feeling on a 1 to 10 scale.

Once you have identified and measured the feeling of the belief you can move on to the next and most important step.

Step Number 3: <u>Use a clearing process</u>.

There are numerous clearing processes to choose from. This is an area where you would greatly benefit from working with a coach who is skilled in helping individuals to break free from limiting beliefs. As a Miracles Coach and personal development coach in general, I specialize in helping my clients to break through the limiting beliefs that have held them back for extended periods of time.

It's important to understand that not all clearing methods are equal. Some may provide temporary relief from intense emotions while not permanently detaching the emotional charge from the belief itself. If you are going to attempt to clear your limiting beliefs on your own, it is important to explore and experiment with various clearing processes. Commit yourself to making a solid effort to find the process that works best for you. I should point out that clearing methods correspond very strongly with a person's learning style. There are great visual clearing methods, auditory clearing methods, and kinesthetic clearing methods. Some clearing methods may also combine two learning styles. Again, it's important to find the method that resonates with you and that you can place belief in. It's very difficult to achieve favorable results if you have any thoughts or feelings of skepticism regarding the clearing method.

Step Number 4: <u>Re-measure the feeling of the belief</u>.

Once you have completed a clearing process it's important to go back and re-measure the feeling and identify any changes in the level of intensity. This is really the only way to know if the clearing process is working for you. I suppose you could just wait and see if you experience any changes in perceptions or behavior. However, the quickest way to determine if you are getting results is by re-measuring the feeling using the technique outlined in Step 2 of Clearing Limiting Beliefs.

Personally, I like knowing that I can get immediate feedback and assess whether what I am doing is getting me the results that I want whether.

Step Number 5: <u>Repeat if necessary.</u>

Step five is pretty simple. I won't go so far as to say it's self-explanatory. Believe it or not, I have had to explain this step to clients in great detail numerous times. If you re-measure the feeling of a belief and find that there is leftover energy, in other words, you didn't completely clear the feelings that were attached to the belief, the next logical step is to go back and do the clearing process again and continue clearing until the emotional level is an absolute zero.

Clearing limiting beliefs takes practice. However, if you commit yourself to the process you will begin to recognize a profound change in your beliefs about yourself, others, and the world around you. Most importantly, clearing your limiting beliefs will allow you to release yourself from victimhood and to create the circumstances you truly desire for yourself.

Take Hedi from Australia, for example. When I first began working with her, she was in such a victim state that she believed she had absolutely no control over any aspect of her life. She was so disempowered that she was on the verge of suicide as a last ditch effort to end the emotional suffering that was the result of her limiting beliefs.

Here's what she had to say in a letter:

"When I came into the Miracles Coaching Program I was really, and yes I do mean really at rock-bottom down in the dumps depressed; and that is an understatement. I so wanted

off this world hoping, that I would not need to wake up, because I did not think I could battle this world much longer. I knew I was down and just barely short of out. I had been hit by non-stop disasters. I experienced at least one major disaster per month for 9 consecutive months and on each occasion adding to the previous disaster. Clearing my limiting beliefs has been extremely necessary. I'm still a work in progress. But, I already have experienced big improvements. I now have hopes and plans for a future, where not long ago I was just hoping to depart from this earth."

Another client named Sharlene had a similar experience with clearing limiting beliefs:

"My circumstances before working with Gregory in Miracles Coaching were horrid. I was ready to commit suicide or at least was thinking about it. My life was very difficult to say the least. I have never felt lower and more unwanted and devalued as a human being as I did when I began working with Gregory.

Through clearing, I overcame limiting beliefs in my self worth and how I thought no one would want me or love me and that I had no personal power. My life has completely changed. I'm making friends and getting respect. I feel love and not hate.

Most importantly, Gregory, my coach, helped me believe in myself again. He held my heart in his hands and took care of me. He made me believe in my own worth. It's ongoing now. My life has completely changed."

Finally, another client named Pearl had this to say about her experience with clearing limiting beliefs:

"I was planning my suicide when I stumbled onto Joe Vitale's Miracles Coaching. Understanding that things happen for a reason, I watched his videos and was so wowed by the 'Seeing yourself in Five Years From Now' concept.

My life up to that time had been bad memories, negative people, bad investments, and a mother that constantly reminded me that I would never be successful. I was definitely not living the life I wanted and was too much in a negative state to turn things around on my own. With the help and nurturing of Gregory, my Miracles Coach, I managed to start turning my life around, eliminating toxic people, and overcoming my Mother's negative put downs. It was difficult, but with the help of my coach and the process of clearing my limiting beliefs - I did it!"

Through these and other experiences, I've come to realize that 'clearing my limiting beliefs' has been one of the most profound miracles in my life and in the lives of those whom I coach. Through the process of 'clearing my limiting beliefs', I have come to love and appreciate myself, to recognize my innate greatness, and to allow myself to be authentic in all areas of my life.

Although clearing my limiting beliefs has been a true miracle, I wouldn't be where I am today had I not experienced the miracle of Feeling Things Into Existence.

MIRACLE NUMBER 4

FEELING THINGS INTO EXISTENCE

                    ❊   ❊   ❊   ❊   ❊   ❊   ❊   ❊

IT BECAME APPARENT THAT THE more time I spent with Joe Vitale in person and on the phone during our monthly masterminds calls, the more I began to internalize and master the principles of the law of attraction. So much of what I began doing as a miracles coach was beyond anything I had ever done previously. And I had been studying and practicing personal development for at least twelve years or more by the time I was first introduced to Joe's teachings. In fact, I became aware of Joe and began following his work at least three years before I officially became a Miracles Coach.

Joe and I share a common obsession for old books about new thought, so the concept of the law of attraction wasn't at all new to me. In fact, my experience with the principles of law of attraction combined with my overall experience with personal development coaching were primary factors in my being chosen as a Miracles Coach. But, Joe opened up a whole new approach to the law of attraction and to manifesting my desired outcomes. He taught me to rely heavily on the art of creative visualization as a means to directly access divine energy. Joe calls this mysterious and nearly mystical approach, Nevillizing.

The first time I had ever heard Joe use the term Nevillizing was in Joe's audio program titled *The Abundance Paradigm.*

Joe coined the term Nevillizing after a master metaphysician by the name of Neville Goddard. Neville was one of the most prolific writers on the topic of metaphysics of what time? In fact, Neville Goddard is probably the only person that has written more on metaphysics and the principles governing law of attraction than Joe Vitale himself. And that's saying a lot.

Most of Joe's followers don't know that he didn't start out as a metaphysician. In fact, he began his career as a copywriter and it was his fascination with the work of famed showman P.T. Barnum that led to his discovery of other books on new thought by the likes of Henry Harrison Brown, Orison Swett Marden, William Walker Atkinson, Thomas Troward, Florence Scovel Shinn, Ernest Holmes, and yes, Neville Goddard, just to name a few. But Joe would go on to be more prolific than every one of them save Neville Goddard.

It was from Neville that Joe learned the practice of feeling as though he was already in possession of the very thing he desired to manifest into his life. Neville used terms such as, "The Law of Imagining" and "Assuming the feeling of the wish fulfilled", or "Feeling into existence."

It was these and other concepts that piqued Joe's fascination for the more metaphysical side of personal growth. So much so that Joe eventually went on to obtain a PHD in metaphysics earning him the affectionate title Dr. Joe.

To me, Joe made everything about business, life, and the law of attraction look so easy. There seemed to be this ease about him. It only takes five or ten minutes in his presence to realize that in spite of his fascination for showmanship, he's really not much of a showman. I mean, there are things he can do that one might consider showy. Things like illusions, sleight of hand, bending pieces of steel, stage hypnosis, and playing guitar are just some of the contents of his vast bag of tricks. But even still, Joe comes across calm, cool, and collected in person. To tell you the truth, I've always figured that because he gets so much done, he must be jammin' on the inside, even though his epidermis may look somewhat bored. But that's just Joe.

Then there are the things we share in common. I play guitar, I'm a hypnotic copywriter, I'm a speaker, I'm a coach, and now, even as I type these words, I have become an author.

So much of what Joe does is what I had dreamed about doing for years. But it wasn't until I learned the real magic of "Feeling into existence" that I began to manifest the exact circumstances that I had imagined so often before. Prior to that it was goal setting, repeating affirmations, dream building, and a lot of hard work.

As far back as my days in college I knew that my life calling was to help people fulfill their divine potential by helping them to overcome the beliefs and emotional patterns that keep them stuck. By the time I began my college career I had already been religiously studying personal growth and development for just over two years. I had conducted numerous, what I call, curbside coaching sessions with friends and acquaintances. Although I didn't have the official title of "Coach", I was already stepping into the role and serving my fellow man.

I started my college career majoring in Mass Communication. Prior to college I often envisioned sharing transformational ideas on a global scale. The majority, if not all, of the speakers and personal development trainers who I had been exposed to up until that point in my journey were clearly master communicators. So, I had this idea that I would combine sharing positive messages through mass media with great communication skills. And there you have it; Mass Communication. It just made sense. I often considered the idea of having a personal development radio talk show. Unfortunately, the college professors I spoke to about my ideas were quick to give me all of the reasons that it probably wouldn't work out in the way I envisioned it. And because I hadn't yet discovered how to overcome my limiting beliefs or to protect my subconscious mind from negative influence, I allowed their limiting beliefs to influence my own, which in turn influenced my decision making process.

One of the most destructive things I have ever done in my life is to believe someone else's opinion about me or about what I imagined was possible for me. It ended up costing me almost six years of progress toward my goal of becoming an agent of change in the lives of others. That's how long it took me to break free from the status quo and begin reaching for my dreams on my own terms. If I could offer any advice or wisdom it would be, "Don't Do That! Don't allow the doubts and fears of other people to become your own doubts and fears." Will Smith (playing the role of Chris Gardener in *The Pursuit of Happyness*) admonished his son not to, "...Ever let somebody tell you can't do something..." He went on to warn him that, "You got a dream you gotta protect it. People can't do somethin' themselves and they wanna tell you - you can't do it. You want sump-em go get it – period!"

My wife and I had been living in Idaho about 6 years as I was getting my formal education and struggling to carve out a decent living. We had a little family of 3 children when I went to work for Clear Channel Radio as an advertising executive. I did ad sales, wrote radio spots, and began what would later become a side gig in voiceover. I was convinced that this was it. I was finally going to realize my dream of becoming an agent of change in people's lives. But just as in college, my ideas and aspirations were met with negative feedback from everyone with whom I shared my ideas, especially my colleagues at Clear Channel. And again, I allowed the doubts and fears of others to become my own doubts and fears. I couldn't see it at the time but looking back on it, I am convinced that anyone with a fair amount of talent represents competition to those who had been around longer or who believed they were somehow more deserving of a promotion than I was. In reality, they had no good reason to cheer me on. Understand that broadcast media is extremely competitive.

Just as with most things I tried and failed at, this turned out no differently. I was in a daily battle with the voice of my father reminding me that I was worthless, that I wouldn't amount to anything, and that I didn't deserve anything. I eventually went into a downward spiral of self-sabotage. Still not yet knowing how to change my beliefs left me with the inability to overcome the adversity that came from within.

"If what I wanted to have happen couldn't possibly happen in the direction I was going, then what was I doing there?" So – I gave up on my dreams for the time being and I quit. When I went in to tell the station manager I was quitting she was quite shocked. I explained that I didn't feel like I was good at what I was doing and that I was taking up a position that could be done better by someone else. She responded by saying that she felt like I was doing a fantastic job and that I was making a mistake by quitting. Not to mention that they were getting so much more than what they were paying for and I know she knew it. I could sell, I could write creative and responsive ad copy, and I had a natural talent for Voice Acting and announcing. What radio station manager in his or her right mind would want to lose someone with so much to offer?

Her response actually came as a shock to me. Yet, I was so caught up in my own negative story that I couldn't accept that I was doing any good at all in the position.

When it came to my career and providing for my family, I proved to be my own worst enemy. In hindsight, I realize that the experience I gained as a copywriter and VO talent was tremendously valuable. I'm convinced that sometimes our perceptions, even if they are negative, are exactly what we need to move us forward in the direction of our desires, even if we can't see it at the time, especially if we're not on the right path. I wasn't on the right path.

I began to realize that if I was going to achieve my life mission, I needed to be in a city that had more to offer. Less than a year after leaving Clear Channel I made up my mind to leave Idaho.

The day I interviewed for a position with The Professional Education Institute was perhaps one of the single most providential and defining days of my life. There I was, sitting in my SUV staring at the huge corporate building that in less than 5 minutes I would be entering for an opportunity to finally seize my dreams. The feeling was surreal. Less than 6 hours before that moment I had received the call from Matt Fowler for a phone interview which ended with him asking when I could be there for an in-person interview. To which I replied, "How about in four and a half hours?" I needed the additional half hour to shower and get into business dress.

I could tell that he was surprised my response. "You mean four and a half hours from now? You want to come down today? That's later than I normally stay in the office but if you're willing to come down, I'm willing to stay late for the interview." So it was settled and just about thirty minutes after the phone call I was showered, dressed to do business, and on the road to Salt Lake City, Utah from Twin Falls, Idaho. As I showered I kept hearing the words of Les Brown ringing in my ears. "You Gotta Be Hungry!"

I made the entire four-hour drive in silence. The only sounds that could be heard were the hum of snow tires on the asphalt and the voices of all of my personal development heroes echoing in my brain. There was Dexter Yager in his raspy voice, "Hey, you can make it! You can do it! Dream big! Believe in yourself! You're a winner!" Zig Ziglar was shouting for me to keep on pumping and not to stop and that, "It's your attitude not your aptitude that will determine your altitude." I really needed that one because deep down inside, part of me was feeling under qualified, yet logically, I knew I had everything they were asking for in the job description and more. I reminded myself that I had made it through the phone screening and was advanced to an in person interview. "Surely Matt Fowler wouldn't let me make the four hour drive if I wasn't qualified or if he didn't see something desirable in me in the phone interview." That's what I had to keep telling myself. Finally, there was Earl Nightingale reminding me that "People with goals succeed because they know where they are going." In that particular moment I knew exactly where I was going, and at this point in my life I was risking everything to get there.

For more reasons than one, the interview ended up being like none I had ever experienced. He began by telling the receptionist that there was no need to give me a tour. Wow. Had I washed out that quickly? Was it already decided that I wasn't even in contention for the position? Was the interview from here on out just going to be a formality?

There were moments when I felt a lot of doubt in the tone of his questions: so much so that I began to doubt any possibility at all of me landing the position. At one point I seriously questioned why I was even there. Quick. I need to do something. But what? I wasn't entirely sure. What could I possibly do to change the course of what I felt was becoming a sinking ship?

When we finally came to the end of the interview, he asked if there was anything else I wanted to add. "That's it! This is my chance to save this ship from sinking and me from ending up in a watery grave of failure and rejection!" So, I sat forward on the edge of my chair, squared my shoulders, leaned forward, and looking Matt Fowler right in the eyes, declared slowly, clearly, and with absolute certainty of what I was about to say, "Your company will be better by my being here." Then I immediately sat back, folded my arms and allowed a slight smile to come across my face. I was pleased with myself.

If I recall correctly, he was somewhat speechless. But I wasn't about to let someone take something that for the first time in my life, I felt I truly deserved. As it turned out, he later admitted that was exactly what he was hoping I would do. That I would reach out and snatch the opportunity and not let a little bit of posture rob me of my certainty about whether or not I wanted the position.

We stood up, walked out the door and immediately he asked the receptionist to give me a tour. He shook my hand one last time, and while still grasping it in his hand said, "You really want this opportunity don't you?" To which I replied, "Absolutely I do." "We'll be in touch," he said. Then he turned, walked away and I was taken on the grand tour.

I had originally planned to stay in the area that night. But, it was the middle of the holidays and I just wanted to be back home with my wife and kiddos. So, I got in my SUV, drove to the gas station to fill up and grab some snacks and a couple of energy drinks, and then made the 4 hour drive back home. I called Hillary from the road to tell her I would be coming home. She was surprised I wasn't staying overnight. I told her I'd fill her in on what happened when I got home. I didn't want to say too much. She had mixed feelings about me driving all that way in the middle of the night and I had mixed feelings about the interview.

When I finally arrived at home she asked how I felt it went. I confessed that I wasn't too sure. "I gave a great interview. But I'm not sure if it was enough to get the job, so I'm not getting my hopes up. I'm just going to wait to see what happens." She understood my feelings, gave me a hug and a great big kiss and with all of the love and support I could have hoped for said, "It will all work out. Whatever is supposed to happen will happen for us."

January 3rd, 2005 was a Monday. The phone rang at roughly 10:00am. The voice on the other end of the line was a 20 something hipster named Jace. Jace was in HR at The PEI. He was calling to let me know I had been offered the job and asked if I would accept the position. I verbally accepted. He said they would send me the offer and other papers by email. I thanked him, hung up the phone, and then I literally cried. It was one of the greatest Christmas gifts I had ever received. From then on, everything was going to change.

Hillary reminded me that I played a role in getting the job too. It was me and what I had to offer that they wanted.

I would be starting my training in two weeks from the day I accepted the position. I had no idea where we would live or what would happen. But, I had seized the opportunity, and deep in my heart I knew that there was divine providence at work. I reminded myself that so many times I had prayed for this, or something very near to it. And now it had arrived. It was knocking on my door. I refused to make the mistake I had made so many other times with so many opportunities. I wasn't going to take counsel from my fears. I wasn't about to turn Matt Fowler away. I refused to send him the stable of my life where I would miss out on this miracle. Oh no. I was going to make room in the inn. A new star was about to appear and I wanted to be sure I was there to see it in all its glory.

Steve Harvey has stated that, "Every successful person including you, believe it or not. Every successful person in this world has jumped... Eventually you are going to have to jump. You cannot just exist in this life... If you are waking up thinking that there's gotta be more to your life than it is, man believe that it is. Believe in your heart of hearts that it is. But to get to that life, you're gonna have to have to jump."

In the moment I told Jace I would accept the opportunity I had jumped. I hadn't heard Steve Harvey say those words. But, I understood the concept and knew I had to jump.

I started in the coaching industry in January of 2005 as a result of one of the biggest leaps of faith of my lifetime. The day I started at the PEI marked the beginning of a new career and a new era. It was also a day that I reaffirmed to God that I was willing to take the leap of faith and follow the path he had laid out for me. And it's a good thing, too, because who knows, I could have spent the next several years in Idaho working some dead end job.

Within a year I was part of the brand new Jack Canfield Success Principles Coaching Team and was awarded Top Producer for 2005.

I'd love to say that the years leading up to becoming a part of the Miracles Coaching team were as amazing as that first year. I wouldn't be telling the truth if I did. I also wouldn't have been blessed with so many life changing lessons were it not for a few, sometimes even severe, wrecks along the way. It was the love and support of my wife that helped me to weather the storms of adversity.

Some of the storms were much worse than others. In fact, one such storm was my own creation. Without going into too much detail I will confess that I made a very poor business decision. A decision that ended up costing over a quarter of a million dollars. In the end, we were forced to sell our beautiful five-bedroom home overlooking Utah Lake. I was so emotionally devastated. At one point I couldn't help but sob uncontrollably telling my wife how I feared I was proving my father right once again. "I can't let him be right. I can't let him be right."

This certainly wasn't anything I had ever envisioned for myself. It was nonetheless a reality. However, I didn't have to allow it to remain as such. After all, I had the power to choose something better. So, three house moves in less than two years and one major life changing decision later, I woke up woke up finding myself on the Miracles Coaching team doing what I have been placed on this earth to do, helping my fellow man overcome the limiting emotions and beliefs that keep him, bound in the chains of mediocrity.

Not all visualization is equal. I had spent countless hours upon hours visualizing the things I wanted in my future never seeing the majority of it come to fruition. And therein was the answer to my problem of not manifesting things the way I had wanted. I always visualized my desired outcomes as something in the future. And ever in the future is where my desired circumstances remained. Until the one day, while listening to *The Abundance Paradigm*, Joe Vitale revealed one simple secret. It was a secret that he learned from Neville Goddard and now I was about to learn the same secret from Joe. "This is the secret," he later on said to me in person, "that is missing from the movie The Secret", the award winning documentary about the law of attraction of which he also happens to be a star. Because of this one simple but profound and powerful principle, my life has never been the same. And now, because I'm revealing the secret right here on this page of my book, you are also going to learn the secret. You'll want to read the following quote several times until the message and its meaning settles deep into your understanding. This is the second most powerful principle I have learned in all of my study of personal development. It has been almost as valuable as learning to clear my limiting beliefs. And now, here's the life-altering secret. Are you ready? Here goes. "Assume The Feeling of the Wish Fulfilled or in other words Nevillize." Did you get that? Here it is again. "Assume The Feeling of the Wish Fulfilled or in other words Nevillize." Now go back and read that a few more times and ask yourself the same thing I asked myself when I first heard it. "What on earth does that mean exactly?" Fortunately Joe explains it very clearly and concisely in the audio. This is basically what he says. Keep in mind I'm paraphrasing, but I'm being careful to include everything you need to take this information and put it to work in your own life the way I have put it to work in mine, the way Joe has put it to work in his, and the way several hundred of my coaching clients have put it to work in their own lives.

Nevillizing is the practice of visualizing your desired outcome while feeling gratitude as though the very thing you desire is already yours or that the very circumstance you wish to experience has already come to pass. This means visualizing your goal as though you are living beyond the outcome and feeling what it would feel like to have reached the goal. The primary feeling should be one of gratitude. In other words, you are not visualizing the moment you achieve the goal, you are visualizing your circumstances *as a result of* the goal being accomplished. Then you attach gratitude to the mental picture as though you are expressing gratitude for what has already happened.

For example, if my goal was to win the Boston Marathon, I would not visualize crossing the finish line, I would visualize thirty to sixty days beyond the finish line and feel gratitude for my accomplishment. This is exactly what Neville Goddard meant what he said the key to manifesting your desire is to,

"Assume the feeling of the wish fulfilled". And this is also what Joe Vitale meant when he coined the term "Nevillize".

For a while I had a hard time attaching gratitude to something that I had not yet manifested. Sure, I could get excited about the prospect of reaching a goal. But feeling gratitude as though I had already reached the goal was very difficult for me. I have had many coaching clients express the same concern.

I began to explore possible solutions to my challenge with visualization. I knew that if I could overcome the challenge, I could teach other people to do the same. The solution that finally came to me was simple, yet very effective.

Rather than trying to directly attach gratitude to the desired outcome, I began to think about the many changes and benefits that I would experience as a result of reaching my goal. Somehow this made feeling gratitude for something I desired to happen much easier. It also resulted in visualizing my outcomes with far more detail as I considered the many ways in which my life and the lives of my wife and children would be blessed as a result of my success.

In addition, I felt inspired to write a letter to myself declaring my success to my friends and family in very much the same way that people send out letters during the holidays sharing highlights from the previous year. However, instead of just sharing highlights, I felt impressed to tell about the previous year in lavish detail. This evolved into a process that I now assign to my coaching clients called, "The Future Letter."

Here's the process.

First: <u>Choose a date in the future as the setting of your letter</u>.

Second: <u>Select your desired outcomes</u>. Basically you identify the goals you would like to achieve.

Third: <u>Categorize your goals</u> as follows. Physical goals (health, wellness, physical activity), mental/emotional goals (beliefs and mental energy), spiritual goals (connection to your higher power and manifestation), business/financial goals, and finally, relationship goals.

Fourth: <u>Begin writing your letter focusing on a section at a time</u>. In each section emphasize the achievement of each and every goal from that specific category and the resulting circumstances and feelings. You don't have to write your categories in any specific order. However, it is very helpful to write about the goals from each category in the same section of your letter. This helps to keep your thoughts and ideas organized. It will also be helpful later on as you begin to use the letter as a visualization tool. I'll explain this shortly.

Once you have completed the letter, be sure to sign and date it in the future on or about the date you picture yourself writing the letter. No specific date is required nor is it even necessary to discuss a full year. It can be as little as three to six months. I chose one year because of the similarity to a holiday letter that details a full year of activity.

The next step in this process is simple.

Fifth: <u>Read your future letter each night for twenty to thirty nights</u> or as long as it takes to commit the essence of the letter to memory. The more detail you can commit to memory the better.

Sixth: Each night as you place your head on your pillow, close your eyes and <u>dwell on the contents of your letter in gratitude,</u> from memory in as much detail as possible as you drift into relaxation and finally into sleep. The longer you can remain in a state of conscious awareness while in a grateful and relaxed state, the more effective this process will be. As you dwell on your letter, remember, you must attach feelings of gratitude to the mental picture of achievement as though it has already come to pass, and inevitably it will come to pass.

The visualization portion of this process is based on a concept found in *Life's Missing Instruction Manual* by Joe Vitale called, "The Night Window." In addition, using the contents of your future letter is a powerful enhancement that I believe makes the process much more powerful and effective.

In Joe's book it states that, "The night window is your chance to place your order. Few know that when they drift off to sleep they are merging with the energy of all that is, what some call the universe. This is your opportunity to place your wish and the universe will fulfill it." He goes on to say that you should, "...Drift into sleep, smiling, trusting, knowing that it will be fulfilled."

Interestingly, medical science has shown that when a person is in a state of relaxation, or *alpha* state, which naturally occurs during the process of falling asleep, there is a bridge that is formed between the conscious and subconscious minds. This bridge makes it possible to program the subconscious mind with very little effort. Nothing more is needed than to visualize your desired outcome with positive emotion. When one enters *alpha state* and then expresses feelings of gratitude, an additional brain wave is produced called *gamma waves*. Some believe that *gamma waves* are the link between human kind and the divine source. Neville Goddard somehow understood this and incidentally taught that "The Night Window" is indeed the most ideal time to engage in creative visualization.

It's important to understand that the subconscious mind only carries out orders. It doesn't argue or debate. It does what it is told to do. By programming your subconscious mind through this process, you exponentially increase the odds that you will achieve the outcome that you desire.

This is the exact process that I followed to become not just a Miracles Coach, but a TOP Miracles Coach. In my work as a coach I receive more positive feedback, higher satisfaction ratings, and more client success testimonials than any other Miracles Coach. This is the same process I followed to be recognized as the Coach of The Year for 2015. This also the same process I followed to land a two book publishing deal after just eleven queries to publishers and literary agents. And it just so happens that it's the same process that I followed to attract the opportunity to co-author this work with Mr. Fire himself, Dr. Joe Vitale.

The experiences that have come through this process are truly too many to list. My challenge to you is to do what many of my coaching clients and I myself have done. Put this process to work right now and experience for yourself the miracles that can occur when you allow yourself to go back to what you were so good at as a child and *pretend* in gratitude that your deepest desires have come to pass in the exact or an even better way than you imagined while drifting into your own dreamland of miracles.

As I mentioned, I receive numerous letters from clients sharing the miracles that happen in their lives. Jose from Italy is an example of what can happen in just two or three months working with me as your coach or even one of my skilled colleagues:

"Probably the most important learning was Nevillizing. A considerable amount of cash arrived to my bank account a consequence of selling my shares of a company to my

business partner. I received 50% more of what was originally on the table.

While working with my coach I managed to sell out the company, which was operating in conflict with my values. When starting coaching I thought this was going to be impossible. I'm very happy to get out of the environment that was energy repressing and psychological depressing. I can feel that the energy is liberated, started to take new shape, and is a fresh breath. It is allowing me to create new circumstances to bring my desires to life.

I have new business opportunities. I was catapulted in a new business sector of incredible potential where I already signed a contract that will make in a month 60% of my year goal. I have met people with whom I'm putting together some other more important deals that will greatly surpass not only the goal set, but much more."

I should point out that money isn't the primary motivation of every client I work with, but let's face it, "Money makes the world go 'round'", so sang Liza Minnelli in the classic Broadway Musical, *Cabaret*. So, as you might have guessed, a number of the letters I receive tell of miraculous money manifesting experiences. Andriana, a client from South Carolina shares how quickly her financial situation changed in spite of facing challenges while working with me as her coach.

"In only one month I could already see so much progress as a result of working with Gregory, my Miracles Coach. I even manifested the money to pay for the coaching program... I felt very positive and excited and I was extremely positive about my financial situation beginning to change... Even though a

couple of financial challenges came up at the time I began, working with a coach was a great decision."

There have been other times when the new client starts out with a high level of skepticism about Miracles Coaching and Law of Attraction in general. Even still, just the idea of working with a coach presents a lot of hope for some people. This is what Zoltan from Seattle said about his experience.

"Before starting with my coach I was very skeptical... But, immediately I knew this time it was different. Something had changed inside me. I had been given, as I look at it now, my last nudge from the universe towards the life I want to manifest... The wealthy, abundant life my divine Creator wants me to have. I have learned many key principles of an abundant lifestyle such as gratitude, manifesting, and clearing my limiting beliefs, and letting go. So far I have been extremely successful, manifesting upwards of $20,000.00 in one month!! I have since relinquished my debt."

I have to use a cliche and mention that the amounts of money mentioned in these experiences are not typical. However, the ability to experience such miraculous change in a short period of time is very common.

Although I've never been skeptical about the power of creative visualization and Nevillizing, as I mentioned earlier in the chapter, for a number of years I took the long route to manifesting the things I desired in life. My intentions were very clear and my attitude was generally one of optimism and enthusiasm. The missing link was consciously bringing my desired future into the now by feeling as though my wish had already been fulfilled.

For many, myself included, the most challenging part of the manifesting process is the final step of Attracting Miracles. However simple it may seem at its core, it's the fundamental difference between chasing and attracting. For me, finding power in the act of surrender came through witnessing the miracle of "Letting Go."

MIRACLE NUMBER 5

LETTING GO

❊ ❊ ❊ ❊ ❊ ❊ ❊ ❊

MY WIFE CAN TELL YOU that I had control issues for the first ten or so years of our marriage. Anything I could control I tried to control along with a good portion of what I couldn't control. It makes sense, though. I grew up in an environment where I had no control over anything. I was told what I could and couldn't wear, eat, say, and sometimes even what I couldn't feel or express emotionally. From there I was thrust into the adult world still being unsure of what I could and could not control. And so, out of fear of being perceived as weak by others, I tried to control everything. I had to "Keep It All together."

To put it mildly, this created some issues along the way.

Without going into too much detail I will say that in 2009 I made a major financial error that resulted in being defrauded out of a substantial amount of money. When all was said and done, we were well past the quarter of a million dollar mark and well on our way to half a million. It sounds like a lot to lose on paper, but the lessons I learned and the greater closeness I gained with my wife and children over the next few years have made it all worth the loss. I have been asked on a number of occasions if I'd do it all over again if it meant learning the same lessons. To which I can truthfully say that if I knew it would end up the way things are now, I'd do it all over again. Maybe not twice. But, at least once more. Things are pretty good where they are now. And let's just say that I'm pleased but not satisfied.

The fraud however, resulted in the eventual sale of our 4,800 square foot five bedroom home that overlooks Utah Lake and included an unobstructed view of Mount Timpanogos. On many occasions passersby would stop and ask if the home was for sale. Which honestly was one of the things I loved about the home and its location. It was a great lot, a great home, with a great view. It may sound silly, but when I would stand on the balcony and look out over the lake and the valley beyond, it felt like I had arrived.

I have to confess that I was driven by material wealth. In my mind, material possessions represented control over my circumstances. By providing my family with a lovely home, nice vehicles, a boat, motorized toys, and other material possessions, I felt as though I was providing them with security. In short, I felt like I had things under control. So you can imagine the blow I felt on the day we signed the papers to sell our home.

When we were finally able to sell the home, we did so at a 60% loss. It was all we could do to pay off the hard money loan I had taken against the home and prevent the home from going to auction. Being paid for in full, we were able to walk away with a small handful of cash. It wasn't enough to be excited about, but was enough to land on our feet and start over.

We had been in the home for almost six years. For our children, finding out we were leaving was emotionally devastating. Not just leaving, but leaving on what seemed to them to be very short notice. Which made it all so much worse. Thankfully, the Moore Family, our closest friends who lived just a block away, moved to Texas about 3 months before we left the neighborhood. This made it a little bit easier for our family to move. But, only a little bit.

Over the next year we moved twice more, had our sixth child (a boy we named Samuel, meaning God has heard, which for us was quite appropriate at the time), and also endured a flood that resulted in the loss of most of our family photos and mementos. That part was especially hard on my wife. I would be willing to bet that part alone was harder than giving up the house.

We eventually settled in a comfortable home that we could rent in a nice neighborhood. The story behind finding the house is one of divine providence. To this day I am very grateful for the many miracles that occurred while living in that home. We liked our neighbors, our new church congregation, and we especially liked the homeschool community of which we had become a part. My wife and I seemed to be on the mend emotionally and we were communicating more closely than we ever had before. Things seemed to be looking up for us. I was even adjusting to being a renter and driving the vehicle I had bought for $2000 through an online classified. Did I mention I also lost my brand new truck? It was the first vehicle I had ever purchased new. Losing it along with the house was rough at first, but with all of the other lessons I was learning, on the surface, I seemed to be working through this one as well.

And then disaster struck.

It was about 7:00am when the phone rang. I woke up and quickly answered the phone in case it was a wrong number. I didn't want to disturb my wife. Having a nursing baby makes any amount of sleep a luxury. So I acted quickly hoping I could answer it before she would wake up. I acted so quickly I didn't notice that she wasn't even in bed. She was already awake and in the shower. It wasn't a wrong number. I wish it was but it wasn't. I can still remember it as though it was just minutes ago. That's one of the curses of having the memory of an elephant.

It was one of the worst phone calls I had ever received beside the ones notifying me of the deaths of each of my grandparents. It was even worse than the call I had received notifying me of the death of my father.

My youngest brother in-law, Tyler, was calling to tell us that my father in-law had suffered a massive stroke and was in ICU. No one was certain if he was going to survive the next 24 hours or even until later that morning and we needed to get to the hospital as soon as possible.

We did what we needed to get packed for the next few days, we loaded my wife's Sequoia, got the kids up and dressed and loaded in to the car, and headed north for a three hour drive to Idaho Falls, Idaho.

It was on the drive that I began suffering a string of panic attacks that lasted nearly a year and a half.

"How could this be happening? Why this? Why now? Couldn't it wait until later? Couldn't it just go away all together?" I had to keep things together for my wife. "Here I go again. I have to be strong. I have to be in control. I thought I had gotten past this crap." I had dealt with some anxiety during the sale of the house and the moves. But I thought I had worked through it all and that was over. Apparently it was back with a vengeance. Over the next three hours I suffered what felt like a non-stop anxiety attack. It's a wonder I was able to keep myself together to drive.

By the time we arrived at the hospital in Idaho Falls, I managed to pull myself together enough to go in and help my wife get situated in the long-term waiting room outside of the ICU. Being surrounded by family and friends was a comfort and helped to ease the overwhelming amount of anxiety I was experiencing. It just wasn't enough to make it go away altogether. Figuring that part out was going to take a while.

I realized three days later on the drive home that I was in for a long haul. The force of the attacks was worse than any I had ever experienced. The prospect of going back to work and having to interact with clients while dealing with such high anxiety was almost overwhelming.

I went back to work the following Monday. After nearly every coaching session I had to do everything I could to pull myself together.

Over the next few weeks I developed insomnia. Even when I finally did fall asleep at night, within a couple of hours I'd be awakened by the intense sensation that I was hanging upside down. I'd wake up instantaneously with my heart pounding as though it would literally rip right through my chest. All I knew how to do at the time was sit and wait for the attack to run its course. Then I'd lay back down and try to sleep again. It was a vicious circle. The lack of sleep led to more severe anxiety and the severe anxiety led to a lack of sleep. The irony of it sometimes made me literally laugh out loud. The whole situation was like something out of a tragic comedy and I was the central character. To make matters even worse, it was the middle of winter and my commute to the office was about fifty miles each way in heavy snow. Yes, part of it was even uphill going both directions.

There were many drives home that I would have to pull off the interstate and call my wife to talk me through the panic. It often helped to gamify my commute, telling myself that if I could just make it to the next exit I would be that much closer to the safety of home. Oddly enough, every evening I would pull into our driveway and almost immediately the anxiety and panic would subside. Hillary would be at the door to greet me and I would relish the comfort and security of her loving and compassionate embrace. Because of my mistakes and the challenges I brought on to my family, I felt undeserving of the blessings I enjoyed. But, I was so grateful to receive them and I was grateful for the grace extended to me by both my wife and by God.

I was never a "Depressed" person. I never understood what it meant to be, "Depressed". I had never experienced "Depression" that I could recall. At least not the way I had heard other people talk about it. The only way I can describe what was happening to me is that I was getting, "Bummed out". The thought that I might end up living out the remainder of my days in a state of constant anxiety robbed me of my zest for daily life. I began adjusting my life to accommodate the anxiety. It got so bad that I was adjusting nearly every activity in my life to avoid anything I suspected might lead to a panic attack. I was pretty much the epitome of a Control Freak at this point.

This must have caught my wife's attention. I think her patience might have worn a bit thin. And what happened next, well, I never saw it coming.

I don't recall exactly what I was saying as we pulled out of our driveway to run errands in town. I do, however, recall what Hillary said. It came out of nowhere and was like nothing she had ever said to me before. Wait for it ----. "You're so full of sh*t!" "Huh?" I was completely gob smacked. Where did that come from? "All day, every day you talk about living in the present and having an attitude of gratitude. You're a hypocrite." "What?" was the only thing that could find it's way to my open mouth. "What are you talking about?" I asked. "When are you going to let go of the past, stop living in the future, and learn to be grateful for where you are right now? You have a family that loves you, I love you, we have a decent home and cars that work, and a career that you love. When are you going to let it all go and enjoy what you have right now?"

Hillary has always been what I call my warm personal enemy. She is my absolute truest friend. Yet, there are times when she is not afraid to serve me up a dose of raw truth. This had been one such time. Apparently it went down with a spoon full of sugar because from that moment forward I began planning my escape from the emotional prison I had carefully built and in which I deliberately confined myself.

I began to take massive action by getting out of the house and taking walks around the neighborhood or going places that challenged me. I began studying mindfulness and engaging in mindfulness meditation on a regular basis. I learned to observe my thoughts, feelings, and emotions and to recognize that what I was experiencing was not *me* but just a false program. By coming into awareness of myself I could quickly dis-identify with every thought, feeling, emotion or body sensation that didn't appear to immediately serve my higher good. I became selective about my experience, which allowed me, for lack of a better term, to begin living in the now. With every good moment and then every good hour and eventually every good day, came expressions of deep gratitude. Until eventually I woke up and realized that the anxiety had left me altogether.

I had learned to live in the present, capable of expressing gratitude for exactly where I was in any given moment. No looping thoughts about the past. No foreboding over the future. I was in full understanding that where I was, was exactly where I was supposed to be at that time in my life and that I had two choices, I could feed the dream, or I could feed the nightmare; it was totally and completely up to me. This was another point in my life where I was choosing to take 100% responsibility.

And then the miracle took place, not all at once or "Overnight" as people say but incrementally, however no less miraculous. I should point out here that as I explain what happened next in my life and the lives of my family, you might become inclined to disbelief. That's okay. I wouldn't at all hold it against you because I probably wouldn't have even believed it myself had it not been for my own experience.

This is how it happened – the condensed version.

Do you remember that fraudulent business deal I told you about; the one that I invested a bunch of money into that eventually led to having to sell our family home? Well, I had almost totally given up on both the civil and criminal processes. I couldn't find a single attorney that would take the case on contingency. With every inquiry came the same response that even if we did win in civil court, the best we'd get is a judgment that may take years to collect if at all. Being basically broke beyond taking care of our immediate needs each month, there was no feasible way to hire an attorney to go to work for us to recover our lost money. Then, as if I had received a calling from God, I became inspired to carry out my own investigation into what happened with the money I had invested.

In the process of my investigation I began close communication with the father of a friend who was also defrauded in the same bunko deal. His father was quite business savvy and together we would brainstorm and come to conclusions as to which immediate actions I should take next. One of the actions I took was based on his experience in the insurance industry. He suspected that the title company to which his son's and my money was wired might have a surety bond to protect them against mistakes that could be made in the process of completing deals. So, I immediately did some research and discovered that they did have a surety bond. In fact, they had two; one of which went into effect the exact day before my money was wired to their bank.

Getting the insurance company to communicate with me was no easy task. But, when they finally did assign an adjuster to the case, the news I was given was, at face value, not very good. They denied my claim, as I had no grounds for compensation. At least not by the company holding the surety bond.

What initially seemed like a light at the end of the tunnel became the light on the front of a fast moving train that was set on a course directly toward my hopes of ever regaining the money that was lost. I almost lost all hope, and this is where the miracle finally took place.

I clearly remember that on the day I learned that my claim was denied, that night before falling asleep, I sat on the edge of my bed and explained to God that I had invested time, money and emotional energy into repairing my mistakes. I had taken responsibility for my bad decision. I had suffered my own personal hell and made my way back among the living again. I had done all I had felt inspired or that I could think to do. Was there anything that could be done? Was there any grace that I could receive? And then, I quietly got into bed, and closed my eyes. Nearly instantly I was overcome with a deep sense of satisfaction and gratitude that I had not given up. I had done what was within my power. I was now handing it over to God, and with the calm assurance that all would go according to God's plan for me, I let it all go and then drifted into a deep and restful sleep.

I awoke the next morning shaken by an unseen force. I sat up in bed nearly startled. A voice came into my mind very loud, very clear, and very concise, as one person speaks to another, "Call The Surety Company. Ask Why They Specifically Denied Your Claim!" Immediately I picked up my phone and dialed the number. When the polite lady on the other end answered the phone, I asked to speak to the adjuster who denied my claim. I was placed on hold. Why was I not surprised?

When the adjuster picked up his phone I quickly introduced myself. I explained that I understood my claim had been denied and that his company didn't owe me anything. I was just calling to ask why they chose to deny my claim. "Oh... That's simple," he said. Then he continued, "Our investigation revealed that while our client may have been involved in one or more crimes, your money was not part of any crime or wrong doing; at least not by our client. In fact, our client never received your money. The account that your money was wired to was seized by the

Nevada State Attorney General's office." "Are you serious?" I asked. "Dead serious," he said. "I couldn't even make that up. So, that's whom you need to call. They've got your money. Anything else I can do for you?" I didn't even know what to say. I felt like I could have kissed him right through the phone. Immediately I hung up and called the Nevada State Attorney General. I explained to the woman who answered the phone why I was calling and asked if she could put me through to the person I needed to speak to. "Can you hold for a moment?" she asked. "Sure, no problem." I said. She placed me on hold. When she returned she explained to me that my case was being handled by one of the assistant AGs and that it was decided they were not equipped to handle that type of case so they contracted with a public sector law firm. She explained that all of the money that had been wired into the account that was seized, which indeed included my money, had gone into receivership. Meaning the money had been seized but was now going to be given back to all of the rightful owners who made an official claim. The end date to make a claim would be the following Thursday. She said I had exactly 48 hours to make my claim or my money would become property of the State of Nevada. She acknowledged that I was on the list but said she couldn't offer me legal advice. She simply asked if I wanted to file a claim with added insistence in her voice as if to nudge me to say yes. "Of course I want to make a claim!" I nearly shouted. She gave me the telephone number of the attorney's office in Las Vegas who was handling the case and the name of the attorney that had been assigned to handle the claims. She insisted that I call them immediately because the deadline was so close. I thanked her profusely and, again, would have kissed her through the phone if I could have.

Miracle Number 5   Letting Go

I hung up the phone and immediately called the attorney's office. They put me through to the attorney that had been assigned to claims process. Again, she confirmed that I was on the list, and confirmed the amount of money that was owed to me. I was told that she could not offer me legal advice but asked if I wanted to make a claim and was reminded that the deadline was the coming Thursday, just 48 hours from the day I was calling. Once again I nearly shouted, "Yes!" and would have kissed her though the phone if I could have.

She confirmed the information they had on hand and said she would send the necessary forms immediately. She confirmed that they had made it to my email inbox. Again, I thanked her profusely and hung up the phone.

I need to point out that not only was I on the list, they and the Attorney General's office had current contact information for me and never, I mean never, so much as sent me a letter or made a phone call to say they had my money all along. Instead, they were banking on the possibility that many of the claimants, myself included, would have no idea where their money had gone and that the money would end up as property of the state of Nevada. How do I know? Because when they sent me the claim forms, it included a list of all claimants. There was a notation next to those who had filed claims and those who hadn't. The number of those who hadn't filed claims was astounding. The total amount of money that would almost certainly go unclaimed was staggering. Under normal circumstances I would have probably been furious. But this was no time or place for negative emotions.

My next order of business was to contact my friend's father and give him the news and instruct him on how his son could

85

make a claim for his money. I even contacted the Utah Securities Division to insist that they notify anyone who had given money to the individuals who had defrauded me. I wanted them to get their money back as well. I wasn't going to allow myself to be the only one to benefit from this miracle.

I filed the necessary papers to make my claim. I received return confirmation and an approximate date that a check would be sent.

Within a short period of time I received a check for the exact amount of my initial investment. A couple months later I received another notice that the judge handling the case recommended that the unclaimed funds not become property of the state of Nevada but that anything over and above attorney's fees be divided up among the claimants based on the percentage represented by their initial investment. This was labeled interest due to the amount of time that the money had been tied up by the government. The judge felt that the money could have been returned much earlier and that the interest was an apology on behalf of the State of Nevada. Then, a couple months later, a final check was sent completely unexpected. It was a considerable amount less, but when all was added up, we had received our initial investment and the amount of interest and fees paid to the hard money lender at the time of closing on our home.

I have to profess that what had happened was nothing short of a miracle. But how, you ask? Well, that part was simple. Not easy, but simple. It was the power of Letting Go.

Now I had something real, something concrete, something profound, something miraculous that I could share with my Miracles Coaching clients about letting go. Sure, overcoming the anxiety was a miracle. I would never discount or dismiss it. And sure, I had experienced numerous other miracles. But getting the money back. That was a miracle that went beyond all reason. It went beyond anything I had done or could do. My biggest contribution was that I was able to Let Go.

It's important to understand that letting go does not preclude you from *taking inspired action*. One of the things I have heard Joe say over and over is that, "The universe loves speed." When you feel inspired to take a specific action, don't wait around. Don't hesitate. Don't second-guess. Don't dismiss the inspiration. Take action right away. Even if the action you take is to write down an idea or an action you will take in the future, write it down. Be sure to include what you felt in the moment you received inspiration. You will need to reconnect with the feeling later on to help you avoid dismissing the inspiration as something trivial or insignificant. Joe has often emphasized that the feeling you experience combined with the inspiration you receive is what propels you forward toward your desired outcome. If you lose touch with the feeling, you may lose momentum or give up completely on your intended outcome.

Miracles Coaching Clients often say that letting go is the hardest part of the law of attraction for them. I've seen many clients complicate the process without even really trying. Rejecting the possibility of life without reaching their goal is the most common hang up. Rejecting a possible outcome is a form of resistance and, "Whatever we resist will always persist."

A common example is being highly resistant to not manifesting money or being in an unhealthy relationship or being flawed in the eyes of others. This results in a feeling of neediness or desperation and prevents the desired outcome from flowing into their life. Instead, the thing they desire retreats leaving their desire unsatisfied. As their coach I strive to make sure they grasp this concept at a fundamental level or they will gum up the process and not get the results they are looking for.

The best way I can describe the letting go process is this – are you ready? Here goes. Letting go means desire without need. Desire without need. Joe says that it basically means that, "I would like to have it happen, but it's not the end of the world if it doesn't happen." You see? It's very simple. But so often people will approach their desired outcome with a feeling of desperation and chase after their desired outcome as though their life depends on it. I wouldn't go so far as to say that one should be indifferent about their desired outcome. But rather, one should be fully and completely grateful for where they are in the moment, recognizing that whether or not they manifest their desired outcome, they are going to be just fine. Remember, I would like for X, Y, or Z to happen, but if it doesn't, it's not the end of the world.

The Miracles Coaching Clients that don't get stuck on this principle often experience life altering miracles in a very short period of time. So to help those who are stuck get un-stuck, there are a couple of exercises I have them do. The first is one I call Radical Gratitude.

Radical Gratitude is actually based on Joe Vitale's pencil experience. While down and out and on the verge of suicide Joe found comfort in, yep, a pencil. As he looked at the pencil he had in his hand, he considered all of the many reasons to be grateful for the pencil. The process goes as follows:

Step 1. <u>Identify something you are grateful for</u>. Preferably something relating to your current situation.

Step 2. <u>List as many reasons as possible to be grateful for the thing you've identified</u>.

Step 3. <u>Read the list of reasons you are grateful ten times per day for the next seven days</u>.

Step 4. <u>Choose a new gratitude week</u>.

There you have it. It's that simple.

The next process requires a bit more effort but is powerful and very effective. It's called Allowing. One of the most effective ways to Let Go is to break through any and all resistance to an outcome that is less than what you truly desire.

I attribute the allowing process to Janeen Detrick. I learned this technique during my first few months as a Miracles Coach. Since then I have assigned it to numerous clients and have received testimonial after testimonial regarding its effectiveness. This is the process:

Step 1. <u>Identify the outcome that you are most resistant to</u>. This is generally the opposite of the outcome you desire. For instance, if your desire is to manifest a large sum of money, the opposite outcome may be to end up in poverty.

Step 2. <u>List all of the feelings or emotions you might experience when considering the opposite outcome of what you desire</u>. For instance you might feel fear, anger, embarrassment, shame, or anxiety.

Step 3. <u>Begin to list the ways you might allow yourself to show up or the perceptions you may hold as a result of either manifesting or not manifesting your desired outcome</u>. See the following example regarding being poor:

I allow myself to be poor.

I allow myself to be afraid of being poor.

I allow myself to be angry at myself for being afraid of being poor.

I allow myself to love myself for being afraid of being poor.

I allow myself to believe that being poor is a weakness.

I allow myself to believe that being poor is a virtue.

I allow myself to be grateful for being poor.

I allow myself to not be grateful for being poor.

I allow myself to hate poor people.

I allow myself to love poor people.

I allow myself to believe poor people are weak.

I allow myself to believe poor people are strong.

I allow myself to not love poor people.

I allow myself to love poor people.

I allow myself to worry about what people think if I'm poor.

I allow myself to not care what people think if I'm poor.

I allow myself to love myself if I'm rich.

I allow myself to love myself if I'm poor.

I allow myself to be loved by others even if I'm poor.

I allow myself to be loved by God even if I'm poor.

My family members love me whether I'm rich or poor.

God loves me whether I'm rich or poor.

And there you have it; the Allowing process. Once you finish your allowing script you will likely experience a sense of peace regarding your desired outcome. Allowing crosses over into the realm of clearing. However, I feel it is most useful when wanting to Let Go of attachments to a desired outcome. You may think of many other statements that might better relate to your unique situation. It's perfectly okay to create your own script in the way that best works for you.

One Miracles Coaching Client Diana shared her experience with letting go:

"I am calmer because I understand there are no mistakes in the universe. I have let go of my need to control everything or every outcome... Allowing continues to be a valuable tool. I have a cheat sheet to use twice a day but I also stop in the day as things come up and create new allowing sentences."

When we Let Go of our need to control outcomes, our confidence in our ability to manifest increases. Sonia shared this experience:

"I have given up thinking about "how" things will manifest. Being grateful for everything I have has enabled me to stretch my thinking and reconsider the amount of my charitable giving—time, goods, and money that I would contribute. I've let go of trying to rid myself of negative people and have put my focus on attracting positive people into my life. Now I really do know that I can be, do, and have anything I'm committed to."

And finally, Umehani wrote to me and expressed her enthusiasm and gratitude regarding Allowing Scripts as part of her Letting Go process:

The ALLOWING SCRIPT and this allowing technique is making a major impact on my life! Seriously major! I have a favorite river spot here in Munich where I throw my notes, wishes or anything I want to. Now when I go there, I feel like I am also becoming like its flow. Somehow I am feeling more connected, more closer to its depth and flow. I hope you understand my compliment for this "Miracles' Coaching by this final statement. I am healing everyday... I LOVE YOU!"

There is so much power to be found in letting go. I have often considered how absolutely counterintuitive it really is. For so long I held the belief that strength was found in control. I have since come to believe that true strength is found in having enough faith and trust in the manifesting process to let go of all attachments to outcomes. By recognizing the many things in my life that I have to be grateful for, I've come to see that there truly is no time like the present.

ATTRACTING MIRACLES

CONNECTING THE DOTS

* * * * * * * *

I KNOW THERE ARE SOME OF YOU who wanted to wade past the story and get into the *how to* part of this book. Sometimes it's just easier to skip over all of the fluff and get right down to the good stuff. Not that my story isn't interesting, but when I say good stuff, I mean the part of the book where I present the Attracting Miracles process in a *connecting the dots* type explanation. Just so you know, I'm okay with that. There's no need to feel guilty or to offer any apology. In fact, I am writing this chapter with you or rather someone like you in mind. His name is Tim.

Tim is a Miracles Coaching Client from Ireland. Tim's entire approach to the Miracles Coaching program is, "Just show me how to make all of this personal development and Attracting Miracles stuff work for me. At the end of the day I'm really just looking for results."

As I've explained to many clients during our coaching sessions, everyone comes into the Miracles Coaching program really looking for one thing and one thing only – Results. Many of my clients have gone through other coaching programs and unfortunately didn't get the results they anticipated. For them, Miracles Coaching has been their final hope before giving up and resigning themselves to a life that is less than what they truly desire.

Before I connect the dots, I want to share an example of the power this process can bring into anyone's life. Because of the nature of the challenges experienced by this couple, I'll just refer to them as H and W. H the husband in this marriage, was just coming out of his eighth marital affair. As far as W the wife was concerned, they were done; the marriage was over. Yet, he had other plans. He had read about Miracles Coaching somewhere online and reached out to Nathan Curtis, one of the senior advisors at Miracles Coaching. Nathan carefully interviewed H in the same way he interviews hundreds of candidates. Nathan carefully selects those whom he feels are the most qualified for the program. During his interview process he is looking for those who are willing to make a commitment of time, those who have a strong desire for and a commitment to change, those who demonstrate a willingness to be held accountable by a coach, and those who are able to make powerful and lasting decisions. He felt strongly impressed that J was a great candidate although his wife would need some strong evidence of change. In the end, she got exactly what she wanted from him and the program. Here are their words regarding their Miracles Coaching experience:

"Our experience with the Miracles Coaching program has truly brought 'miraculous' results. We believe the initial call from Nathan Curtis was a divine intervention. It has changed our lives and the relationship we have with

each other in ways we never believed possible. We were on a fast track to becoming a broken couple and family. At the beginning of our journey, we were on empty emotionally and spiritually. Our marriage had little to no communication and we avoided each other as much as possible. We were shut down and looking for a way out. Divorce proceedings had already been started, but we knew it wasn't what God wanted. Deep down, neither one of us wanted it either. We had visited three different counselors and spiritual advisers, all of who told us they had never advocated divorce until they met us. Needless to say, we had given up. We decided to give the Miracles Coaching program a chance, hoping for our own miracle.

Our coach Gregory Downey gave us the tools we needed to pick up the pieces and move forward. By accepting the 'black marks' from the past, one day at a time we are slowly progressing toward a God-centered more spiritually connected relationship. We are communicating our needs and feelings frequently and honestly, and negatives are becoming positives. Our family is at the top of the to-do list.

Although we are a work in progress, our developing communication skills paired with an attitude of acceptance for each other are a direct result of our training with Coach Gregory. He was a perfect match to us and we will forever be grateful for his kind and patient heart. His knowledge of God's design for marriage has given us the tools necessary to develop and maintain our future together.

There is no doubt that without the help and guidance of our Miracles Coach our marriage and our children's lives

*would have been forever torn apart. Stability and peace
of mind has been restored in our family. We believe we can
live a life of love, peace, and happiness. We will experience
Miracles!"*

Yes! Eight – marital - affairs. It just goes to show that miracles
can and do happen with this process. Keep in mind, much of the
following information is explained in the previous chapters.
However, if you are one of the individuals who skipped ahead to
this chapter, the information will be new to you. I will tell you
though that you are missing out on some of the best parts of this
book. If you are one of the more patient people who has poured
over each line and chapter as I know you have, well, we'll just
say that it won't hurt you to go through the information a second
time. After all, repetition is the mother of skill. Now let's take a
look at the process step by step:

Step 1. <u>Be Clear About What You Don't Want.</u>

For a lot of Miracles Coaching clients this step feels really
counterintuitive at first. However, this is the first step to
empowerment and a life of miracles. I say counterintuitive
because it goes against what they have heard or read from
so many law of attraction gurus out there who preach near
avoidance of any acknowledgement of the things you don't want
in your life. They teach this out of fear that by even mentioning
the things you don't want you might somehow attract everything
on your don't want list, which couldn't be further from the truth.

In reality, by avoiding all of the things you don't want, you're
much more likely to attract them into your life. Avoidance is a
form of resistance, and what we resist ultimately will persist. So,

from my point of view and based on my understanding, by listing the things you don't want, you are actually validating them and releasing the avoidance energy associated with them.

So many people, myself included, have been at a stage when they felt as though life was just a series of events over which they have no control. Not only is it extremely disempowering, it's also the foundation of the *victim state* that prevents a person from exercising their power of choice.

Take a few moments to list the top 10 to 15 things that you don't want in your life. When you list out the top 10 to 15 things that you don't want, you begin to realize that you have the power to choose. Either you choose to continue down the path that produces all of the things you don't want, or you choose to go down the opposite path that offers you everything that you do want.

As I explain in chapter one, by listing the things you don't want in life you are in essence drawing a line in the sand. You are making your declaration of ownership of your life. Your declaration might sound something like this, "From this day forward, I will fearlessly acknowledge the things that I do not want in my life and I choose to forever turn away from the that road which leads to getting more of the things that I have confidently declared that I do not want."

Once you have made your list of things that you don't want, ask yourself, "Why am I still experiencing this in my life?" The answer to your question is generally the belief behind the experience. Write the answers to this question for each item in a notebook or journal. You'll want to refer back to your answers in step 3.

Step 2. <u>Be Clear About What You Do Want</u>

The second step in the process leads to even further empowerment. Once you have decided that you no longer want to continue down the path that produces more of what you don't want, you are free to choose what you do want instead.

Just as you made the list of things you don't want, make a list of 10 to 15 things that you do want. Once you've completed your list, ask yourself the following question for each item: "Why haven't I manifested this into my life yet?" Write the answers to the question in a notebook or journal. The answers to the question will nearly always be the belief that is preventing you from manifesting the things that you do want in your life. You will want to refer back to the answers in step number 3.

Step 3. <u>Identify and Clear Your Limiting Beliefs</u>

Clearing Limiting Beliefs is the process of ridding your subconscious mind or your inner being of the emotional and energetic attachments to beliefs that don't serve your higher good. Clearing Limiting Beliefs is done by applying one or more clearing methods.

Clearing limiting beliefs can be broken down into 5 simple but effective steps.

Step number 1: <u>Identify The Limiting Belief</u>.

The easiest method that I share with my coaching clients to identify their limiting beliefs can be summed up in a review of steps one and two of the Attracting Miracles process. Refer to the Don't Want and Do Want lists and the follow up questions that you wrote down.

The answer to the questions, whether they sound like reasons or an excuse, are generally the belief behind the issue that is either preventing you from ridding your life of the items on your Don't Want list or manifesting the items on your Do Want list.

Step number 2: <u>Identify and measure the feeling that is attached to or giving energy to the limiting belief.</u>

By measuring the feeling on a scale from 1 to 10, you can quickly identify the level of emotional energy that is associated with the limiting belief.

An easy way to measure the feeling is to close your eyes and look downward toward your naval. While placing your attention on your naval, state the belief out loud 3 to 4 times giving yourself enough time in between statements to observe any feelings that might come to the surface. Should any feeling surface, make a mental note of the intensity of the feeling on a 1 to 10 scale and where the feeling is located in your body.

Once you have identified and measured the feeling of the belief you can move on to the next and most important step.

Step Number 3: <u>Use a clearing process</u>.

There are numerous clearing processes to choose from. This is an area where you would greatly benefit from working with a coach who is skilled in helping individuals to break free from limiting beliefs. As a Miracles Coach and personal development coach in general, I specialize in helping my clients to break through the limiting beliefs that have held them back for extended periods of time.

It's important to understand that not all clearing methods are equal. Some may provide temporary relief from intense emotions while not permanently detaching the emotional charge from the belief itself. If you are going to attempt to clear your limiting beliefs on your own, it is important to explore and experiment with various clearing processes. Commit yourself to making a solid effort to find the process that works best for you. I should point out that clearing methods correspond very strongly with a person's learning style. There are great visual clearing methods, auditory clearing methods, and kinesthetic clearing methods. Some clearing methods may also combine two learning styles. Again, it's important to find the method that resonates with you and that you can place belief in. It's very difficult to achieve favorable results if you have any thoughts or feelings of skepticism regarding the clearing method.

Step Number 4: <u>Re-measure the feeling of the belief</u>.

Once you have completed a clearing process it's important to go back and re-measure the feeling and identify any changes in the level of intensity. This is really the only way to know if the clearing process is working for you. I suppose you could just wait and see if you experience any changes in perceptions or behavior. However, the quickest way to determine if you are getting results is by re-measuring the feeling. Use the same technique as described in step 2.

Personally, I like knowing that I can get immediate feedback and assess whether what I am doing is getting me the results that I want or not.

Step Number 5: <u>Repeat if necessary</u>.

Step five is pretty simple. I won't go so far as to say it's self-explanatory. Believe it or not, I have had to explain this step to clients in gross detail numerous times. If you re-measure the feeling of a belief and find that there is leftover energy, in other words you didn't completely clear the feelings that were attached to the belief, the next logical step is to go back and do the clearing process again and continue clearing until the emotional level is an absolute zero.

Clearing limiting beliefs takes practice. However, if you commit yourself to the process you will begin to recognize a profound change in your beliefs about yourself, others, and the world around you. Most importantly, clearing your limiting beliefs will allow you to release yourself from victimhood and to create the circumstances you truly desire for yourself.

Step 4. Visualize Your Outcomes With Feeling

This is the process that Joe Vitale refers to as Nevillizing, a term he coined after the late Neville Goddard.

Nevillizing is the practice of visualizing your desired outcome while feeling gratitude as though the very thing you desire is already yours or that the very circumstance you wish to experience has already come to pass. This means visualizing your goal as though you are living beyond the outcome and imagining what it would feel like to have reached the goal. The primary feeling should be one of gratitude. In other words, you are not visualizing the moment you achieve the goal, you are visualizing your circumstances *as a result of* the goal being accomplished. Then you attach gratitude to the mental picture as though you are expressing gratitude for what has already happened.

For example, if my goal was to win the Boston Marathon, I would not visualize crossing the finish line; instead I would visualize 30 to 60 days beyond the finish line and feel gratitude for my accomplishment. This is exactly what Neville Goddard meant when he said the key to manifesting your desire is to, "Assume the feeling of the wish fulfilled."

For a long time I had a hard time attaching gratitude to something that I had not yet manifested. Sure, I could get excited about the prospect of reaching a goal. But, feeling gratitude as though I had already reached the goal was very difficult for me. I have had many coaching clients express the same concern.

I began to explore possible solutions to my challenge with visualization. I knew that if I could overcome the challenge, I could teach other people to do the same. The solution that finally came to me was simple, yet very effective.

Rather than trying to directly attach gratitude to the desired outcome, I began to think about the many changes and benefits that I would experience as a result of reaching my goal. Somehow this made feeling gratitude for something I desired to have happen much easier. It also resulted in visualizing my outcomes with far more detail as I considered the many ways in which my life and the lives of my wife and children would be blessed as a result of my success.

In addition I felt inspired to write a letter declaring my success as though to my friends and family in very much the same way that people send out letters during the holidays sharing highlights from the previous year. However, instead of just sharing highlights, I felt impressed to tell about the previous year in lavish detail. This evolved into a process that I now assign to my coaching clients called, "The Future Letter."

Here's the process.

First: <u>Choose a date in the future as the setting of your letter</u>.

Second: <u>Select your desired outcomes</u>. Basically you identify the goals you would like to achieve.

Third: <u>Categorize your goals</u> as follows. Physical goals (health, wellness, physical activity), mental/emotional goals (beliefs and mental energy), spiritual goals (connection to your higher power and manifestation), business/financial goals, and finally, relationship goals.

Fourth: <u>Begin writing your letter focusing on a section at a time</u>. In each section emphasize the achievement of each and every goal from that specific category and the resulting circumstances and feelings. You don't have to write your categories in any specific order. However, it is very helpful to write about the goals from each category in the same section of your letter. This helps to keep your thoughts and ideas organized. It will also be helpful later on as you begin to use the letter as a visualization tool. I'll explain this shortly.

Once you have completed the letter, be sure to sign and date it in the future on or about the date you picture yourself writing the letter. No specific date is required nor is it even necessary to discuss a full year. It can be as little as three to six months. I chose one year because of the similarity to a holiday letter that details a full year of activity.

The next step in this process is simple.

Fifth: <u>Read your future letter each night for twenty to thirty nights</u> or as long as it takes to commit the essence of the letter to memory. The more detail you can commit to memory the better.

Sixth: Each night as you place your head on your pillow, close your eyes and <u>dwell on the contents of your letter in gratitude</u> in as much detail as possible as you drift into relaxation and finally into sleep. The longer you can remain in a state of conscious awareness while in a grateful and relaxed state, the more effective this process will be. As you dwell on your letter, remember, you must attach feelings of gratitude to the mental picture of achievement as though it has already come to pass, and inevitably it will come to pass.

The visualization portion of this process is based on a concept found in *Life's Missing Instruction Manual* by Joe Vitale called, "The Night Window." In addition, using the contents of your future letter is a powerful enhancement that I believe makes the process effective.

In Joe's book it states that, "The night window is your chance to place your order. Few know that when they drift off to sleep they are merging with the energy of all that is, what some call the universe. This is your opportunity to place your wish and the universe will fulfill it." He goes on to say that you should, "...Drift into sleep, smiling, trusting, knowing that it will be fulfilled."

Trusting and knowing that it will be fulfilled is the core of step number 5.

Step 5. <u>Letting Go</u>

Miracles Coaching Clients often say that letting go is the hardest part of the law of attraction for them. I've seen many clients complicate the process without even really trying. Rejecting the possibility of life without reaching their goal is the most common hang up. Rejecting a possible outcome is a form of resistance and, "Whatever we resist will always persist."

A common example is being highly resistant to not manifesting money or being in an unhealthy relationship or being flawed in the eyes of others. This results in a feeling of neediness or desperation and prevents the desired outcome from flowing into their life. Instead the thing they desire retreats, leaving their desire unsatisfied. As their coach I strive to make sure they grasp this concept at a fundamental level or they will gum up the process and not get the results they are looking for.

The best way I can describe the letting go process is this – are you ready? Here goes. Letting go means desire without need. Desire without need. Joe says that it basically means, "I would like to have it happen, but it's not the end of the world if it doesn't happen." You see? It's very simple. But so often a person will approach their desired outcome with a feeling of desperation and chase after their desired outcome as though their life depends on it. I wouldn't go so far as to say that one should be indifferent about their desired outcome. But rather, one should be fully and completely grateful for where they are in the moment recognizing that whether or not they manifest their desired outcome, they are going to be just fine. Remember, I would like for X, Y, or Z to happen, but if it doesn't, it's not the end of the world.

The Miracles Coaching Clients that don't get stuck on this principle often experience life altering miracles in a very short period of time. So to help those who are stuck get un-stuck, there are a couple of exercises I have them do. The first is one I call Radical Gratitude.

Radical Gratitude is actually based on Joe Vitale's pencil experience. While down and out and on the verge of suicide Joe found comfort in, yep, a pencil. As he looked at the pencil he had in his hand, he considered all of the many reasons to be grateful for the pencil. The process goes as follows:

Step 1. <u>Identify something you are grateful for</u>. Preferably something relating to your current situation.

Step 2. <u>List as many reasons as possible to be grateful for the thing you've identified.</u>

Step 3. <u>Read the list of reasons you are grateful ten times per day for the next seven days.</u>

Step 4. <u>Choose a new gratitude each week.</u>

There you have it. It's that simple.

The next process requires a bit more effort but is powerful and very effective. It's called Allowing. One of the most effective ways to Let Go is to break through any and all resistance to an outcome that is less than what you truly desire.

I attribute the allowing process to Janeen Detrick. I learned this technique during my first few months as a Miracles Coach. Since then I have assigned it to numerous clients and have received testimonial after testimonial regarding its effectiveness. This is the process:

Step 1. <u>Identify the outcome that you are most resistant to.</u> This is generally the opposite of the outcome you desire. For instance, if your desire is to manifest a large sum of money, the opposite outcome may be to end up in poverty.

Step 2. <u>List all of the feelings or emotions you might experience when considering the opposite outcome of what you desire.</u> For instance, you might feel fear, anger, embarrassment, shame, or anxiety.

Step 3. <u>Begin to list the ways you might allow yourself to show up or the perceptions you may hold as a result of either manifesting or not manifesting your desired outcome.</u> See the following example regarding being poor:

I allow myself to be poor.

I allow myself to be afraid of being poor.

I allow myself to be angry at myself for being afraid of being poor.

I allow myself to love myself for being afraid of being poor.

I allow myself to believe that being poor is a weakness.

I allow myself to believe that being poor is a virtue.

I allow myself to be grateful for being poor.

I allow myself to not be grateful for being poor.

I allow myself to hate poor people.

I allow myself to love poor people.

I allow myself to believe poor people are weak.

I allow myself to believe poor people are strong.

I allow myself to not love poor people.

I allow myself to love poor people.

I allow myself to worry about what people think if I'm poor.

I allow myself to not care what people think if I'm poor.

I allow myself to love myself if I'm rich.

I allow myself to love myself if I'm poor.

I allow myself to be loved by others even if I'm poor.

I allow myself to be loved by God even if I'm poor.

My family members love me whether I'm rich or poor.

God loves me whether I'm rich or poor.

And there you have it; the Allowing process. Once you finish your allowing script you will likely experience a sense of peace regarding your desired outcome. Allowing crosses over into the realm of clearing, however, I feel it is most useful when wanting to Let Go of attachments to a desired outcome. You may think of many other statements that might better relate to your unique situation. That is perfectly okay to create our own script in the way that best works for you.

Hopefully by having the Attracting Miracles process laid out step by step, you'll be able to work through the process in a way that allows you to clearly see the results of each step.

When going through this process, it's very important that you suspend all other programs or processes that you might be doing. "Why should I do that?" You ask. The answer is very simple. This is what I call the "3 Pills" dilemma. Let's say that I'm a physician and you come to me complaining of a pain in your knee. In response to your complaint, I diagnose your ailment and prescribe a pill that is sure to resolve it. You then leave my office, pill in hand, and return home to find 2 of your friends waiting on your doorstep for your arrival. Each of them has heard about your ailment and has come to offer you a pill that is also certain to cure your ailment. Not wanting to offend either of them, you graciously accept their pill and over the course of the next few days you take the two pills along with the one you received from me. By the end of the week the pain is gone and your ailment appears to be resolved.

Upon returning to my office, I ask how the knee is doing, to which you respond, "Fantastic! The pain is gone." My natural assessment would be that the pill worked. However, your explanation is one of uncertainty. Because you took 2 pills along with the pill I prescribed, you have no sure way of knowing which one is responsible for your results; thus the "3 pills" dilemma.

The purpose of sharing the Attracting Miracles process is to give my readers a set of actions that is specific and the results of which are measurable and repeatable. If a person is engaged in multiple processes, it's almost impossible to measure specific outcomes from each process. So, it's important that you stop whatever other processes or programs you are using so that you can make a clear connection between action and outcome.

People tend to be skeptical by nature. Seeing specific results from each of the five steps will create confidence in the Attracting Miracles process and help you to stay committed to the process long enough to get results. It will also ensure that at any time in your life, you can apply the Attracting Miracles process with near certainty that you will attract your desired miracle.

How much more certain will you be knowing that you now have a nearly foolproof set of tools that allow you to create the life you desire in a step by step connect the dots sort of way? The only thing that could be more powerful than what you've been given in this chapter is having the opportunity to have me or another Miracles Coach guide you step by step through the Attracting Miracles process. Coaching isn't for everybody, but those who do work with a miracles coach typically see results much sooner than they will following the five steps to Attracting Miracles on their own.

I encourage you to commit yourself to this process. Put each step to the test. The only thing you have to lose are the old perceptions, emotions, beliefs, and behaviors that have kept you stuck in a life, that until now, has been less than what you truly deserve.

My Secret Life

A Miracles Coach

❋　❋　❋　❋　❋　❋　❋　❋

H E WAS TALL, BROAD IN THE shoulders, and heavier set. Almost certainly the result of a life sustained on meat and potatoes. His handshake was as firm as his demeanor and his edges were as rough as the rock and sagebrush filled landscape from which this man sprang. His speech was folksy and filled with references familiar only to those with roots common to his own. It took me months to figure out what was meant by the term Honyock. He was exactly what one might expect of a man from the small farming community of Oakley, Idaho, if they knew what to expect. Unfortunately I had no idea what to expect, which led to my regularly being caught off guard by his unwarranted gestures of tough love. He often seemed far more tyrannical than tender; treating me as though I had committed some act of sin, though it was clear fact that I hadn't. Yet from his mouth flowed words of wisdom that forever left an indelible mark on my immortal soul. Butch Poulton: the one man with whom my memories will forever be forced to endure a love-hate relationship.

For Butch Poulton, personal development was a way of life. It was just short of being a form of religion. In fact, he would often weave together the principles of each as he would teach in monthly training meetings. It was done in such an artful way that I became convinced that one could not reach their full potential without one or the other. True, I had been exposed to a number of ideas and concepts relating to human potential, starting with *Jonathan Livingston Seagull*, then on to the countless Anthony Robbins Infomercials I would watch on late night television. But this is how I developed an insatiable appetite for books and audios on the topic of personal growth and development.

Of all of the concepts I had gleaned from his teaching, none has served me more that the power of belief. It was from Butch Poulton that I came to understand that both fear and faith could not simultaneously occupy the same space within me. He taught that faith is a power that can be wielded like a sword on life's battlefield. For someone who had committed two years of life as a full time agent of change as I had, that principle would produce profound results day after day after day. And though at times I would leave his presence feeling a bit beat up mentally and emotionally, I always went away with a desire to be better and to do more to raise myself to a higher standard of excellence.

It came as no shock to discover years later that Oakley, Idaho as well as a number of his teachings were the two things he shared in common with the late Jim Rohn. The fact that I was even associated with this man was the result of a string of almost unbelievable miracles.

From a very young age I was programmed to believe I would never amount to very much in my life. Had it not been for Jerry

Borchelt, I probably wouldn't have amounted to anything at all. But it was what I had felt the day he kept me in the classroom during lunch hour that gave me the courage to seize opportunity when it presented itself. And so at the age of nineteen, I took hold of the opportunity to radically reinvent myself totally and completely from the inside out.

The year previous was one of the worst I had ever experienced. Looking back, I realize now that it was exactly what I needed to get enough leverage on myself to make lasting change. As I mentioned in chapter three, if someone had told me at eighteen that by twenty one I would be helping others to transform their own lives, I would have written you off as insane if I didn't actually smack you around a bit for being a wise guy.

It's important to understand that with change of lifestyle came a change of environment and relationships. Many people I had known and spent time with saw me so differently in just a few months time that they no longer wanted to associate with me. Apparently if I wasn't smoking, drinking, and using drugs I wasn't much fun to be around. Others were tied to so many painful memories that it made being around them almost unbearable. It began to just make sense to put my time and energy into the relationships that had come to serve my highest good.

The most important of those relationships was with a family by the name of Bellville. Peter, Judith, Anna, Kay, Emily, Justin, Benjamin, Serena, and at the time, little baby Brock (Anna's son). Knowing my situation and recognizing that my current living arrangement was unhealthy, they decided as a family that it would be best if I came to live with them, and so they arranged an empty bedroom for me and sent Justin to collect me and my things. From then on I was accepted as a member of their family. Not because of blood, but because of love. As it is taught in the book *The Education of Little Tree*, I was Kin which meant I was someone with whom they shared an understanding; and that where there is understanding there is a love that goes beyond just being a blood relative.

And so, I disappeared into my new life. I maintained limited contact with some of my family and a couple of my closest friends. But, even one of my closest friends eventually went his direction as I went another.

Leaving California and spending two years back East made it easy to focus on becoming the person that I felt that God had meant for me to be. However, leaving the new family I had come to love so deeply and who had done so much to help me change and grow was difficult. The whole experience was bittersweet. Mom and Dad B made leaving easier by handing me back my house key telling me to, "Hang on to it so you always know you have a home to come back to."

It was a good thing I went because it was while I was away on the East Coast I met Hillary, who I married just five short months after returning to live in California..

As torn as I was about my feelings for Butch Poulton, nearly immediately after arriving back in California, I began once again to honor the commitment I had made to him to continue on in my pursuit of excellence and to dive into anything I could get ahold of on the topic of personal growth and development. One of the first things I got ahold of was an audio program by Zig Ziglar. I'd listen to it while out delivering newspapers for a few dollars until I could find something more permanent and a whole lot more lucrative. Within a short period of time I had landed a job traveling up and down California selling advertising to physicians, other health care practitioners, and health related businesses. I didn't enjoy the travel as much I had anticipated, but the time on the road provided a lot of opportunity to put my undivided attention into studying personal growth and development. It didn't take very long for me to gain a strong conviction that I was being called by God to the speaking and training industry. I knew little if anything about personal coaching at the time. I just knew that I wanted to do what Zig Ziglar was doing or something very near to it.

A few short months later, Hillary had returned from the East to her home state of Idaho. After a lengthy courtship of about two and a half months, we married and settled in Stockton, California. Being a newlywed and having a job that required travel didn't suit me very well, so I left the advertising industry and went into door-to-door sales. I sold pest control for company owned by a man named Dale Bell. He was demanding and pushed me to stretch myself. But, was also kind hearted, fun loving, and very generous. The money I made working for Dale was above average for a twenty three year old newlywed with no children and the perks were many. I naturally rose to the top of the sales team and in turn reaped the benefits of Dale's belief that if you take good care of your employees, they will take good care of your business. In spite of all the walking and knocking on doors, I put on about fifteen pounds working for Dale. He was always handing me gift certificates to eat out and to see movies and such. Life was good as a newlywed who was able to comfortably get by on less than 30 hours per week and all of the perks I could handle.

Being in his employ offered me the opportunity to continue my daily study of personal development and to put the things I had learned over the past two and a half years to work. More importantly, it helped to increase my belief in what I was learning and to believe in myself, in my God given talents, and also to believe in the principles I was so diligently studying.

My desire to answer the call to help others intensified so much so that at the end of the selling season, I gave my notice to Dale and made the decision to attend college in Pocatello, Idaho. Dale made me an offer to stay that I nearly couldn't refuse. There have been times that I wished I had accepted. But I have come to understand that it wasn't the path that God had prepared for me.

Moving to Idaho would once again put a lot of distance between so many of the people I had known previous to my transformation and myself. It made it easy to continue on with little or no association. And being married and part of my wife's family offered new relationships, especially the relationship between my grandfather in-law, my father in-law, my brothers in-law, and me; and obviously my relationship with Hillary, my wife. Keep in mind this was prior to the advent of social media making it easy to slip away into near obscurity.

As I shared earlier, I started my college experience majoring in Mass-Communication. Although I loved learning, what I enjoyed more than being in a classroom were the real work experiences I had in broadcast media. I didn't see any sense in waiting around until after graduation to try landing a job in my field of study, so I took advantage of opportunities in sports information, government and media relations, campus news, and campus radio. This led to my first real job in radio at KSEI doing traffic, weather, and headlines. I was actually part of the first fully produced drive-time radio news program in the South Eastern Idaho Market. I take pride in the fact that like Les Brown, I was "Hungry". That's what Les Always says. "You Gotta Be Hungry!"

After two years of university, I became disenchanted with my school experience. Money was tight more often than not and I came to the conclusion that if I was going to earn enough to support my wife and I, part time gigs weren't going to cut it. I put my education on hold and took a job selling Kirby Vacuums door to door.

My employer at Kirby was an original character. He'd been in sales nearly his entire adult life. He had no college education to speak of, but he was brilliant, and the man could sell a ketchup-popsicle to a woman in white gloves. He was an insanely talented businessman. And what I liked best of all about Delwin Thompson, is that he loved to dance and would often show off a move or two during training meetings or when we were just hanging around having a bottle of water in between demonstrations.

I spent countless hours on the road with Del in his Chrysler van listening to all of the greats in personal development. Zig Ziglar, Les Brown, Brian Tracy, Jim Rohn, David Schwartz, and Lou Holtz just to name a few. As we drove from Pocatello north to Idaho Falls or south to Preston, Soda Springs, or Logan, Utah I would close my eyes and imagine being on stage telling my story and sharing life-changing information. Although I was only with Del for about a year, he taught me some of the most valuable principles I ever learned about preparation, presentation, and persistence. "Don't ever let yourself be defeated mentally." "Things always seem worse when you're not putting your heart into what you love." "If they like you, they'll love your product." At one point he nearly had me sold on taking over his dealership when he was ready to retire. But as you probably guessed, I wasn't meant to be a vacuum salesman for the rest of my life; and so I bid Del farewell, and with my wife, moved to Twin Falls, Idaho to continue my education and to be closer to my wife's family.

I spent the next 7 years working, studying, and preparing for my big opportunity. And then it happened. I got the Job at Legacy Learning (now The Professional Education Institute) the home of Jack Canfield's Success Principles Coaching, Covey Leadership and Personal Development, and Rich Dad Coaching.

Looking back on things, I realize now that I didn't give a lot of explanation about what I was going to do and why it was so important that we leave Idaho and I take the job in Salt Lake City. I suspect it was because any time I tried to discuss coaching with other people in Twin Falls, they always asked me what sport I was going to coach. Even when I did try to explain Personal Coaching they would just tilt their head to the side and give me a confused look as though I had a 3rd eye on my forehead. So, I just quit trying to explain and went foreword mostly keeping my interest in personal development to myself.

Once I was in Utah and working on the Jack Canfield Team my relative secrecy about what I did for a living didn't change much. Hillary understood what I did based on things I'd share about my experiences with coaching clients, but even more than myself, she didn't really know how to explain it to others. Again, it wasn't like she could explain what I did the same way that she might be able to explain that I was a physician, which might I add, was what I spent most of my time in college studying to become. I had somehow convinced myself that to really help people, I needed letters after my name. After all, people listen to doctors, right? So, Hillary, like myself, did what came easiest. She just never brought it up. If someone asked, she would answer that I was a personal coach and people just sort of dropped the subject after that.

What's ironic is that the person who helped me come to the conclusion that medicine was not my life calling was a very successful orthopedic surgeon who knew very little about Personal Development Coaching. What he did know was that I was put on this earth to change lives and that having the letters MD after my name would never add anything more to my credibility than the tremendous adversity that I had overcome earlier in my life. That, in his opinion, was all of the credibility that I would ever need to be able to help a person understand that they are a divine creation and full of infinite potential.

So that's just the way it was. I never really explained to people what I did for a living and neither did Hillary. It was always just a sort of unintentional secret that in all honesty I didn't pay a whole lot of attention to. And then, one day, while talking to my wife, I confessed feeling a bit put off that no one seemed to know what I did for a living and that I rarely had conversations about my work as a coach outside of my circle of colleagues and my closest friends Tyler and Jerry. My mother in-law didn't even seem to really know what I did for a living. So while she would mention my brothers in-law from time to time on social media, I noticed that she never mentioned me or what I did to make a difference in the lives of others. And then it happened again. My wife leveled me with another dose of raw truth. "You can't blame my mom for not knowing what you do or not saying anything about it to anyone. It's not like you've ever really gone out of your way to explain it to anyone. I think you just assume that people should know what you do and when they don't, you allow yourself to be put off and annoyed by it."

I couldn't help feeling a bit guilty for not being more open with people about being a coach. I don't know what I was afraid of or if I was even afraid at all. I think I was still living in the experience of having to give people a full education about what it is to be a personal development coach and for some reason that always just seemed to bother me. I suppose I missed out on a lot of opportunity to serve those around me more fully in ways other than what was expected through Church or some of the other activities in which we are involved as a family. Which is funny because even at church and within other organizations, the majority of people had no idea that I'm a personal development coach until fairly recently. For about the last year I have made a concerted effort to promote myself as a coach through social media, at church, in our service organizations, and even in casual conversation.

By now I've reconnected through social media with many of the people from whom I had distanced myself. Their reactions to discovering that I am a top coach in the personal development coaching industry are often ones of shock and surprise. After all, I was one of the kids that was looked upon by many of my peers as a goof off, a rebel, and one who was least likely to succeed. It's ironic that there are some who will say thing like, "I always knew you would do big things." There are only a handful of people from my past that I would ever believe should they say the same thing.

It's important to me that people understand that I am who I am in large part because of my identity as an agent of change or, in short, as a Miracles Coach. It's important that those who knew me all those years ago understand the damage that can be done through their judgments of others. Part of me wanted to tell my story to help people understand that you never know what potential lies beneath the surface of another human being. So I decided that I would not remain silent and that this part of my life would not go with me to my grave in secrecy.

It was a single experience that inspired me to tell my story because I know that by doing so it will open the door to infinitely more opportunities to use my experiences and gifts to bless the lives of others.

It was about this time a year ago that Hillary and the kids and I were visiting her family in Idaho. My mother in-law and I were talking about some of the recent changes in their community when I sensed she was triggered by some of those changes. I casually mentioned that I sensed she had some strong feelings about the changes and perhaps her feelings were tied to a limiting belief. She asked what I meant by a limiting belief. I responded by explaining that a limiting belief is any belief that holds us back from experiencing joy and happiness or that keeps us in a state of victimhood or suffering. Surprisingly, she agreed that she probably was and that it had been bothering her for quite some time. I then cautiously inquired as to what she had tried doing to overcome the strong feelings that had been keeping her in a victim state. She confessed that she hadn't done very much as she wasn't quite sure what to do. Then I saw it. This was my opening. This was chance. "I'd like to play a little game with you." I said. She hesitated a bit. "Okay?" she replied. "Close your eyes and allow your head to fall slightly." I then asked her to state the belief out loud three or four times and to observe any feeling or emotions that came up in the process. Once she identified the feelings that were feeding the belief, I asked her to measure them on a scale from 0 to 10. Her feelings about the situation were a solid 10. I then proceeded to take her though an NLP clearing process that I use almost daily with my Miracles Coaching Clients. In a single clearing process we were able to take her feelings about the belief from a full 10 down to a 0.

I sat with my mother in-law silently observing her sense of surprise with what had just transpired. Then, all at once, her eyes widened as wide as they possibly could.

She looked as though the windows of heaven had opened and she had received the answers to life, the universe and everything. And then from her mouth came ten of the most satisfying words I'd ever heard her say. "Oh my gosh – That's what you do for a living!" I just grinned and said, "Yes. That's what I do for living." After a brief pause she looked at me and then in the same way one might respond to a light bulb coming on in their brain said, "Ya know, that could be really helpful for people." I just smiled again and in a voice laden with contentment said, "Hmm. You don't say."

THE STORY OF MIRACLES COACHING®

BY DR. JOE VITALE

＊　＊　＊　＊　＊　＊　＊　＊

I STILL REMEMBER THE MOMENT I received the inspiration to create Miracles Coaching®.

It was more than ten years ago. I was visiting the offices of a company then delivering a program of mine on Hypnotic Marketing. That one was designed to help people get into business online. It was enormously successful but I felt something was missing from it. I noticed that some people would sabotage their own success. You could tell them what to do, but they'd do it differently, justify it, and fail. I wondered why.

As I reflected over my own life, I wondered what the single element was that lifted me from despair to success. I had been homeless in Dallas in the late 1970s. I had lived in poverty in Houston for ten years. Throughout it all, I did the right things. I meditated, affirmed, visualized, read books, listened to audios, and saturated myself with the message of success. Still, it evaded me. Why?

I was a take action guy, working on articles, projects and books, praying for a breakthrough. I knew my mission was to inspire people. I knew my calling was to be an author. But why was it all such a struggle? Why were there so many sleepless nights, and days filled with intense stress? What was I missing?

My persistence and hunger kept me motivated, but there were times of hopelessness. There were periods of despondency. I wondered if I would ever make it as a published author, let alone make my living from my words. I kept at it, and there were little successes along the way. I saw a play I wrote produced and it won an award in 1979. I made no money but it was a milestone in a struggling career. It gave me hope. I had my first book published in 1984. It didn't sell well, and I was discouraged. The "big one" was yet to come. It would be another ten years before I saw another glimpse of success. It just seemed to hide from me.

And I had no idea why.

Then, one day, I met a fellow at a social gathering who said he was a coach. I thought coaches were for little league baseball. I hadn't heard that people hired a coach when they felt stuck, or needed accountability and more. I was interested but I was broke. That fellow saw something in me and gave me my first coaching session as a gift.

It changed my life forever.

I've written about that coach in my bestselling book, *The Attractor Factor*. It's when I saw my life open and success start to come to me. It's also where I began to realize that we all need a coach. Without one, we live out of our unconscious beliefs and never know it. That's what I discovered. My lack of success was due to me, not outer circumstances. When I changed me, my outer world changed. Book deals came. Clients came. Money came. Success came.

I've worked with many coaches since, and I still do today. I know that I don't know it all, and that I can't make deep changes without help. Someone other than me, who can listen objectively and lovingly, can help me see my own unconscious beliefs. And change them.

But I also saw limitations within the programs most other coaches and coaching companies offered. While I did break down inner barriers with the coach I worked with, I also noticed that he had limitations in his life that he couldn't see. I ended up leaving him to work with other coaches along the way. But even most of them seemed ignorant of processes I knew and taught, and most were more focused on whatever was the latest self-help fad, rather than focusing on tried and true methods of transformation. And almost all of them seemed to miss an underlying philosophy of spirituality and unlimited living. They certainly seemed oblivious to the "counter intention" methodology I taught and practiced. And I knew that was *the* secret to change.

From time to time, I would personally work with people as their coach. At first I just did it for friends. In time I did it professionally. It was a way for me to test and perfect my methods. It was fun to see clients' eyes light up as they had "a-ha!" moments of insights. It was even more exciting to hear of their successes and have them share them with me. People who had struggled for years were melting blocks and achieving results. I was a proud "parent" to their success.

But as my own success climbed into and out of orbit, I could no longer make time to help people as their personal coach. I was simply too busy. When I appeared in the movie *The Secret*, my life changed forever. I was traveling around the world, speaking to mega groups, appearing on radio and television, being filmed for more movies, and of course writing more books, recording more audio programs, and so much more, including becoming a self-help singer-songwriter and recording numerous albums. I barely had time to feed the cats let alone coach individuals.

I decided to create my own coaching program, articulate my methods, and train my own coaches. It would be the best way that I could truly help the most people. It would be a standout program, like no other coaching service in existence. And I would have ambassadors of it actually do the coaching, rather than me, so I could remain free to inspire people through my books, talks, songs and more.

So, when I was in the hall of the offices of the company then running my marketing program, and one of the managers there asked me, "Do you have an idea for another program?" I was ready.

Without hesitation I said, "I've always wanted to offer one called Miracles Coaching®."

I went on to explain that it would use my methods for getting clear of limiting beliefs, and it would focus on people having a spiritual life of material success. I went on to say that unless we help people clear up what I call "counter intentions," they will most likely not achieve the major success they want, whether in areas of money or health or romance or anything else. They would self-sabotage their own success and never know it.

I said that "counter intentions" are the key; they are the unconscious beliefs knocking out our conscious intentions. I wanted to offer a new kind of coaching; one where people worked on the inside of themselves first. I knew that when you lined up your conscious and subconscious mind, success was almost immediate, and was certainly easier.

Right then and there I decided to announce Miracles Coaching® to the world. The response was immediate and people's successes were astounding. Regular people like you and me, after struggling with issues for years to a lifetime, were achieving breakthroughs.

Miracles Coaching® was the key.

Miracles Coaching® was born.

Miracles Coaching® was a success.

And it still is a success. Given that the program has been around for more than 10 years as I write this, I am proud to say it's doing what I envisioned. You can see some of the proof at www.MiraclesCoachingProof.com

I of course know all the miracles coaches, including Gregory, the author of this book. They are each hand picked and personally trained by me. They have their own extra talents in helping people, but their foundation is the one I teach and preach: miracles are possible for each of us.

All you need is your own willingness - and your own Miracles Coach.

APPENDIX

Experience an Attracting Miracles Consultation:

❀ ❀ ❀ ❀ ❀ ❀ ❀ ❀

I HOPE YOU HAVE FOUND the information in this book entertaining, inspiring, and helpful to you in your efforts to Attract Miracles into your life. The principles in this book have not only changed my life but have changed the lives of thousands of others around the world.

Read what this amazing Miracles Coaching Client had to say about their experience in the Miracles Coaching Program:

"It's been a pleasure working with you as my Miracles Coach. You have helped me so much!

When I began my coaching I was struggling with issues such as self-esteem, anxiety, depression, and weight gain. I've been through an amazing transformation. Issues I have struggled with ALL my life have been resolved.

We did a lot of clearing in our sessions. I practiced the clearing in between sessions and tapped into the resources provided to me by my Miracles Coach. I learned how to cope

with my anxiety and panic disorder, and I am losing the weight I had gained due to self-esteem issues.

My mindset has changed entirely. It was like someone flipped a switch and I came out on the other side a new person. We worked on Success Principles, Law of Attraction and Relationship skills. I have more than achieved my goals for personal development. That was the main focus of my sessions with Gregory. We did a lot of crisis management. He helped me by providing me with resources to overcome the feelings of personal failure in my life.

I have overcome my limiting beliefs through clearing techniques. I am now able to see my way clear to improve my finances. I feel very confident that if I can overcome a lifetime of self-esteem issues, I can attract great wealth. I will continue to do my clearing so that I can maintain the immense progress I have made in my personal development.

For the first time in my marriage of 46 years, I feel worthy of my husband's love. My relationship with my husband is now amazing. It's like it was when we first met. All those years of suffering through low self-esteem, depression and anxiety attacks are now gone. This has been such a huge change for me that I am so grateful for. My marriage has been rejuvenated. My husband is also tremendously grateful.

My Gratitude Journal is added to everyday."

Thank you, Suzan S.

Are you excited to become the next Miracles Coaching Client like Susan to share your Success Story?

Appendix   Experience an Attracting Miracles Consultation:

As a special thank you for reading this book, I'd like to personally invite you to take the enjoy an Attracting Miracles Consultation. This FREE consultation will help you determine whether or not working with a Miracles Coach one on one or in a group setting is the right choice for you.

Simply Visit www.ToBeDetermined.com/Consultation and fill out a brief questionnaire.

Once you have submitted your Attracting Miracles questionnaire one of our friendly Miracles Coaching Advisors will contact you to review your questionaire and provide you with a FREE one on one Miracles Coaching Consultation. The Attracting Miralces Questionaire is the doorway to a world of miracles.

Miracles Coaching isn't for everyone but it just may be for you!

Thank You For Reading.

Miraculously,

Gregory Downey

About Jerry Borchelt

✵ ✵ ✵ ✵ ✵ ✵ ✵ ✵

JERRY BORCHELT HAS DEDICATED HIS entire teaching career since 1972 to teaching at Hanna Boys Center in Sonoma Ca.

When I would visit Jerry's classroom at the end of the school day, there would always be some boys hanging out playing guitar or maybe learning how to play chess. He always always encouraged them to use their minds.

Over the years we have gotten phone calls from former Hanna boys thanking him for all he has done for them. Sometimes there would be a phone call from a boy who had moved on to another school, asking him to help with a math problem. He would teach them over the phone. To this day, our doorbell will ring...."Excuse me, is Mr. Borchelt here? I use to go to Hanna."

Well, lets jump ahead to 2016. This wonderful 70 year-old man is still dedicating his life to the Hanna Boys.

He looks a little different. He has a little less hair, the same mustache and now a beard. He used to get in trouble from Msgr. O'Connor. So, he got a doctors note saying that he couldn't shave because of sensitive skin and now has tattoos on his arms representing his family and his years of education. One of those tattoos is the Hanna Hawk Mascot.

Why do those boys respect and love him? You would have to ask them. It could be that he was a good listener. That is one of the reasons I married him. I truly believe it is because he shows he genuinely CARES. Sometimes you just need someone to listen and to CARE.

Jeanie Borchelt (Wife of Jerry Borchelt)